...THE...
WRIGHT
SISTER

THE
WRIGHT
SISTER

KATHARINE WRIGHT
& HER FAMOUS BROTHERS

RICHARD MAURER

SQUARE
FISH

ROARING BROOK PRESS
NEW YORK

To Betty

Page 1: Orville Wright takes off from a field near Dayton, Ohio, 1904.
Page 2: Katharine Wright in the mid-1890s.
Pages 2–3: Orville aloft in the 1905 Wright flyer.
Pages 4–5: Katharine (with binoculars) views a flight by Wilbur in France, 1909.
Pages 6–7: Katharine (left) washes dishes with her friend Harriet Silliman, 1899.

Copyright information and
Library of Congress Cataloging-in-Publication Data
appear on page 128.

CONTENTS

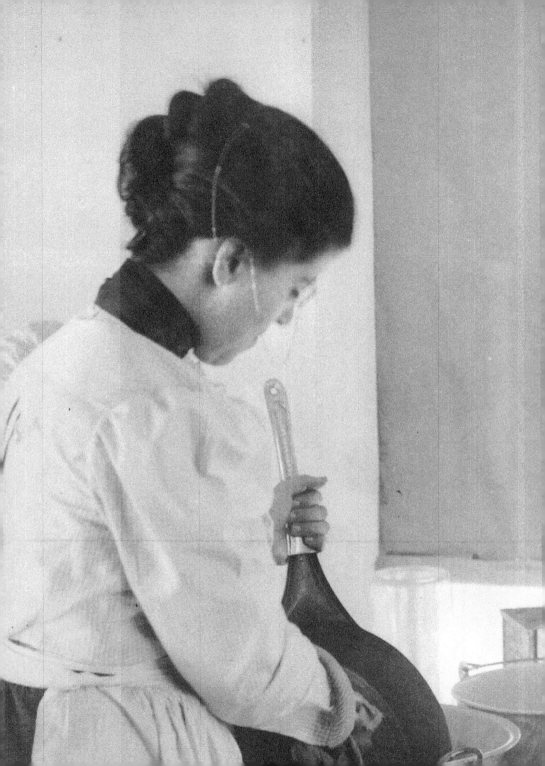

She had been forced into prudence in her youth,
she learned romance as she grew older.

JANE AUSTEN, *Persuasion*

PART ONE ⚭ *December 17, 1903*

Katharine, 1898.

Previous pages:
Wilbur watches as Orville makes history's first controlled, sustained, powered flight —
Kitty Hawk, North Carolina, December 17, 1903.

Dayton

ONE DECEMBER DAY IN 1903 a young woman finished the Latin lesson in her underheated classroom, dismissed the students, and started home.

Though it was only noon, Katharine Wright's teaching duties were over for the day. Just starting were the shopping, housekeeping, and other chores that were hers by virtue of being the woman in charge of a house full of men.

Katharine was the youngest in the family. Her two oldest brothers, Reuchlin and Lorin, were married and living on their own. Her other brothers, Wilbur and Orville, were out of town. Only her father was at home at the moment, but he was a handful. Her mother had died when Katharine was fourteen; she was now twenty-nine and had been running the house in her mother's place ever since.

She stepped into the brisk air. The sun had climbed halfway up the sky, just above the brim of her hat, and it shone brilliantly off the frozen river that ran by Steele High School. Given the season, the day would be short—only a few more hours until night fell on Dayton, Ohio.

Katharine's after-school routine sometimes included lunch downtown or a long walk when the weather was nice. Usually she had to rush home to see to her father's needs. Milton Wright was a bishop in the Church of the United Brethren and a demanding parent.

For some reason, on this day she lingered downtown. It might have been to buy Christmas presents, or to visit friends, or to do errands. But by the time she finally reached home, just after dark, she would find that her life had changed forever—though she wouldn't realize it until much later.

Katharine was called Kate by her friends. To her father she was Katie,

Daughter, or Tochter (German for daughter). To her brothers she was Little Sister, or Swesterchen (German for little sister) — Swes or Sterchens for short.

She was a few inches over 5 feet, neither slender nor heavy, and she moved with spirit. She had long, dark hair done up in a schoolmarm bun. She wore pince-nez glasses — the type that clip to the bridge of the nose. She wasn't considered pretty, but her lively and pleasant manner gave her a special attractiveness.

She had once had an offer of marriage, though it hadn't worked out. Now a husband seemed out of the question. "You are most of my hope of love and care if I live to be old," her father had written her years before, when her mother was sick. He had never remarried and assumed that she would not marry either. As a woman of twenty-nine, she knew that her time was running out. A friend had recently given her a book called *Middle Aged Love Stories*. Sometimes happy, sometimes sad, these tales hinted that life could still hold surprises. Even after the fever pitch of youth had died down and weary routine had taken over, exciting things could still happen. Even so, Katharine didn't expect anything exciting to happen to her.

She had a teenage helper, Carrie Kayler, who eased the housekeeping burden. But there was another burden she had to face on her own: her discouraging career. A female schoolteacher could expect a lifetime as a second-class professional. Already a male colleague had refused to let her teach the Greek courses, which were reserved for the better students. Katharine could look forward to an unending succession of first- and second-year Latin classes, never advancing very far into the fascinating realm of ancient literature that she loved so much.

There were also Wilbur and Orville to think about. Will and Orv, as she called them, were both in their thirties and seemed destined for permanent bachelorhood in the sisterly care of their dear Sterchens. A decade earlier they had branched into bicycles when their printing business started to get dull. Now they were deep into a new interest — flying machines.

Katharine had first noticed this passion four years earlier, when she returned from a college reunion with her old roommate Margaret Goodwin. Normally Will and Orv would have been perfect hosts to Margaret. But this

Orville Wright, 1905.   *Wilbur Wright, 1905.*

Bishop Milton Wright, about 1900.

time they were hopelessly distracted by flight information, newly arrived by mail from the Smithsonian Institution in Washington, D.C.

Will and Orv rarely took vacations, but soon they were writing the U.S. Weather Bureau for advice on locations for flying experiments. In the fall of 1900 they traveled to Kitty Hawk on the coast of North Carolina—almost a thousand miles from Dayton—where strong winds and soft dunes made gliding experiments reliable and reasonably safe. Their plan was to test a means of controlling a glider in flight, believing that their approach would eventually lead to a powered machine that could take off and fly with the grace of a bird.

On their first trip to Kitty Hawk, Wilbur wrote his father letters full of assurances that he and Orville had "no intention of risking injury to any great extent, and no expectation of being hurt"; that they would "not attempt new experiments in dangerous situations"; that the danger was "much less than in most athletic games"; and that "carelessness and overconfidence are usually more dangerous than deliberately accepted risks."

All the talk of injury and danger probably left Bishop Wright more concerned than ever. But he did nothing to stop his boys; and they were as good as their word, for every year from 1900 on they returned safely from lengthy trips to North Carolina, full of new insights into the challenging art of imitating the birds.

As Katharine made her way home that December day the boys had been in Kitty Hawk for nearly three months—their longest trip yet. This time, they were rigging a motor to their glider to create a vehicle that could lift itself into the air under its own power. Others had tried the same thing, but without success. In October and again in early December, a flying machine designed by the head of the Smithsonian, Samuel P. Langley, had attempted to take off from a launching barge near Washington, D.C. Large audiences had watched in dismay as both attempts failed disastrously.

Katharine's journey home took her through downtown Dayton, where the old part of the city nestled into a bend in the Miami River. Then she turned onto Third Street, crossed the river, and continued in the direction of the Wright Cycle Company, where Will and Orv's assistant was minding the store until the boys returned. She turned south into a neighborhood of small

*Amid great publicity, Samuel P. Langley's flyer plunges into the Potomac River
after launch from a barge at right, December 8, 1903.*

The Wright home, 7 Hawthorn Street, Dayton, Ohio, about 1900.

houses and made her way to 7 Hawthorn Street, six blocks from the river. From Steele High School the trip took about half an hour by foot, a little longer by streetcar.

When Katharine walked through the little gate, up the steps, and into the side entrance, she expected to find Carrie in the kitchen fixing supper and her father upstairs in his study. But on entering, she saw that both were standing just inside the door, looking at a piece of paper.

Disbelief

ILTON WRIGHT had given his sons a dollar when they left for Kitty Hawk, saying, "Now let's hear from you when there is any news!" He meant, "Send a telegram so the family won't have to wait a week or more for a letter!"

Telegrams were expensive, about a penny a word; so when Orv finally had something to report, he was brief. Thirty-four words were tapped out in Morse code at the U.S. government weather station at Kitty Hawk, the only telegraph service available. The signal traveled 60 miles by wire to the government office in Norfolk, Virginia. There, the operator translated the dots and dashes into words and read it over the phone to the Western Union operator across town. Orv's message didn't concern government matters, so it had to switch to a commercial service at this point. The Western Union operator converted it back into dots and dashes and transmitted it to Dayton, where it was finally typed up, with mistakes, and taken by messenger to 7 Hawthorn Street.

Milton was holding it when Katharine walked in. Not an excitable man, he was nonetheless smiling as his daughter took the message and read:

KITTY HAWK NC   DEC 17
SUCCESS FOUR FLIGHTS THURSDAY MORNING ALL AGAINST
TWENTY ONE MILE WIND STARTED FROM LEVEL WITH ENGINE
POWER ALONE AVERAGE SPEED THROUGH AIR THIRTY ONE
MILES LONGEST 57 SECONDS INFORM PRESS HOME #####
CHRISTMAS.   OREVELLE WRIGHT

Orville's name was misspelled, the time was supposed to read fifty-nine seconds, and the last part of the message was garbled. But the meaning was crystal clear: Will and Orv had done something remarkable. Four years of tinkering and four trips to Kitty Hawk had produced a machine that could lift itself off the ground and fly through the air under the control of its pilot, something no vehicle had ever done.

RECEIVED at

170

176 C KA CS 33 Paid.   Via Norfolk Va

Kitty Hawk N C Dec 17

Bishop M Wright

7 Hawthorne St

Success four flights thursday morning all against twenty one mile
wind started from Level with engine power alone average speed
through air thirty one miles longest 57 seconds inform Press
home phips Christmas .   Orevelle Wright   525P

"Success . . ."

To top it off, the boys would be home for Christmas, which especially
pleased the bishop. Meanwhile, there was work to do. "Inform press" was the
signal for the family to spring into action.

At Orville's instruction, Milton had prepared a description of the flying
machine along with brief biographies of the inventors. Katharine told Carrie
to hold supper while she delivered this information and the telegram to her
brother Lorin, who lived four blocks away. He would notify the newspapers.
After this errand Katharine stopped at the telegraph office to relay the good
news to Octave Chanute, an elderly flight enthusiast in Chicago who was an
avid supporter of the boys. Then she came home for a celebratory supper
with Milton, made all the happier by the anticipation of a holiday reunion a
few days away.

Later they heard from Lorin that Dayton's most prominent newspaper editor was not even interested in the story. "Fifty-seven seconds!" he had scoffed. "If it was fifty-seven minutes it might be worth talking about." The man was apparently under the impression that Will and Orv had made a balloon flight — hardly a newsworthy event. Not realizing the mistake, Lorin said nothing to clear up the facts.

But even with the facts, the truth was still hard to grasp. No one except a few bystanders at Kitty Hawk had seen the flights, and most of them were not entirely sure *what* they had seen. When a Norfolk reporter tracked down witnesses, they gave such confusing accounts that his newspaper took the easy way out and concocted a fantastic tale that would sell papers. The front page article in the *Norfolk Virginian-Pilot* for December 18 appeared under the dramatic headline: "FLYING MACHINE SOARS 3 MILES IN TEETH OF HIGH WIND OVER SAND HILLS AND WAVES AT KITTY HAWK ON CAROLINA COAST."

Three miles was a wild exaggeration for the longest flight of the day: 852 feet. The story continued with an outlandish description of the flyer, a storybook portrait of the brothers, and a heroic quote to suit the occasion: "Eureka," Wilbur reportedly said at the end of his phenomenal ride.

The fact that none of it was true didn't stop dozens of other papers from printing versions of the story. Readers probably reacted the way they usually did to breathless accounts of unprecedented events: they didn't believe it.

Although the brothers tried in vain to correct the errors, they weren't overly alarmed by the widespread confusion and disbelief. They simply moved on to the next step in their project — improving the flyer.

Meanwhile, the other members of the Wright family went back to their own lives — frustrated with their efforts as publicity agents but still certain that Will and Orv had done something important. For Katharine, Christmas vacation had been pleasant, if hectic. As January snows set in, she returned to her underheated classroom.

PART TWO ❧ *Taking Off*

Susan

ATHARINE WRIGHT was born upstairs at Hawthorn Street on Orville's third birthday, August 19, 1874. Wilbur was seven at the time. Lorin was twelve. Reuchlin was thirteen. Susan and Milton Wright were forty-three and forty-five. Katie would be their last child.

The children paired off by age, as children often do. Reuch (pronounced "roosh") formed a big boys' gang with Lorin. Orv and Katie had a little kids' club. Will, in the middle, sometimes joined one outfit, sometimes the other. Eventually, he grew closest to Orv and Katie.

"No family ever had a happier childhood home," Katharine reminisced years later. Susan Wright was part of the reason. "Mother was a regular genius," recalled the daughter. "[S]he could make anything — and make a good job of it, too. She made sleds for Reuch and Lorin when Father was a country preacher and they had a hundred and fifty [dollars] a year. . . . She was the most understanding woman. She recognized something unusual in Will and Orv, though she loved us all just the same. She never would destroy one thing the boys were trying to make. Any little thing they left around in her way she picked up and put on a shelf in the kitchen. When they remembered the thing again, and would ask for it, she would tease them by asking where they had left it. Orv always left his in the 'pump trough.' And then she would go and get the little contraption."

Young Katie was certain that she lacked the mechanical aptitude that Will and Orv had inherited from Susan. But Orv insisted that she just lacked self-confidence.

When Katie was not quite seven, her mother fell ill. It began as a cough and gradually grew worse. One night she started coughing blood, confirming

Previous pages:
Katharine (back to camera) joins her
friends Harriet Silliman and Agnes
Osborn for a carriage ride, about 1899.

Right: Katharine, age four.

Below: Elementary school in Dayton,
1880s. Katharine is in the front row,
second from right.

23

Susan Wright in her fifties.   *Milton, about age fifty.*

Milton's worst fear: tuberculosis. The disease was widespread at the time and usually started when spores of tuberculosis bacteria were inhaled and lodged in the lungs. Many who were exposed never got sick, but others slowly wasted away as the infection first attacked the lungs, then spread to other parts of the body. There was no cure.

With Milton traveling much of the time, the children took care of Susan and each other. Will cooked and did the laundry. Orv and Katie washed dishes, pumped water, fetched firewood, filled and cleaned oil lamps, and saw to the other endless chores of keeping house. Reuch and Lorin were starting their own adult lives at this point, but Lorin did what he could to be a parent to his little sister. Before school each day he brushed and braided her hair, and he tried to calm her adolescent fears about her appearance: "What is the matter with your face?" he wrote her after he had moved away. "You spoke about something being the matter with your skin but you did not say what."

By 1886, when Katie was twelve, Susan was bedridden. Katie and Wilbur took turns caring for her nearly constantly. Two years later Milton wrote in his diary: "Susan more unwell from week to week." Even then, she managed to hang on for another year. At four o'clock in the morning on July 4, 1889, Milton found her sinking rapidly. She died that afternoon. She was only fifty-eight. "Thus went out the light of my home," he recorded that night.

Lorin was shocked to hear of his mother's death. "[A]lthough I knew that she was very weak," he wrote his father from Kansas, "I did not have an idea that she was dangerously ill. . . . No one ever had a better Mother. . . . [T]ell poor little Katie to write."

Milton

THE YEAR 1889 was doubly difficult for Milton. Not only was his wife dying, his church was coming apart. With a membership topping 200,000, the United Brethren were now bitterly divided over whether members should be allowed to join secret societies such as the Masons. Bishop Wright held that secrecy and exclusionary practices were anathema to the democratic principles of the Brethren. But many of Milton's younger colleagues felt that Masonic-style clubs served a valuable purpose and that church members should be permitted to belong if they wished.

During 1889 the church officially split over this issue. Milton was in the minority and started his own sect that adhered to the old policy. He remained its stalwart leader until he stepped down in 1905.

Bishop Wright was equally rigid with his children. When he was away on church business, Katie could count on letters with passages such as, "I am especially anxious that you cultivate modest feminine manners and control your temper, for temper is a hard master." Sometimes he showed a father's tenderness. After Susan's death, Katie went to stay with relatives and Milton sent her a heartfelt note: "Home . . . seems lonesome without you. . . . But for you, we should feel like we had no home."

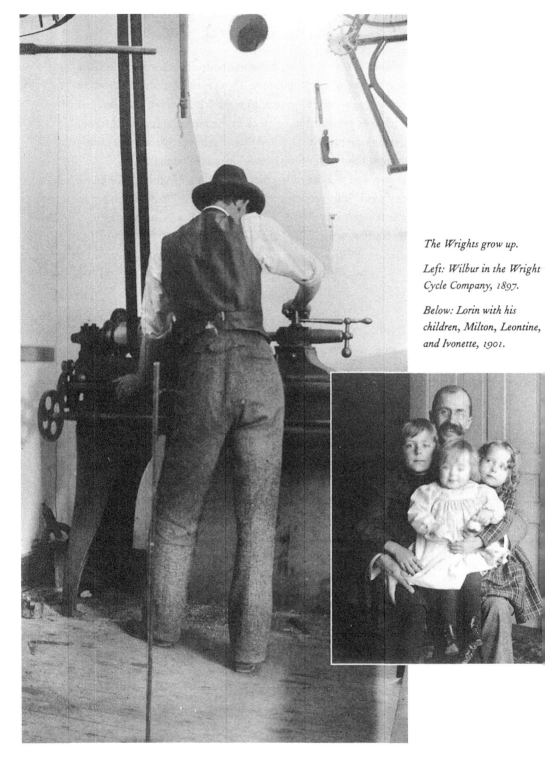

The Wrights grow up.

Left: Wilbur in the Wright Cycle Company, 1897.

Below: Lorin with his children, Milton, Leontine, and Ivonette, 1901.

Milton knew that his daughter, not yet fifteen, was devastated by her mother's death. He did what he could to help her find something constructive to do with her sadness — a way to turn grief into a memorial. It was summer, and he suggested that she collect flowers and press them in an album. Each delicate blossom would remind her of Susan — of her beauty and fragility. Katie followed this advice and kept the album always.

One of Katie's school readers had a story that also affected her for life. It told how all the people in the world were invited to bring their "griefs and calamities, and throw them together in a heap." Then each had to choose someone else's hardship to take away in exchange. One man traded his chronic pain for another's undutiful son. Someone else swapped a long face for a short one. Gray hair went in exchange for skin sores. In the end, though, no one could bear to live with the new problem and wanted the old one back again. Taking the lesson to heart, Katie vowed never to be dissatisfied with her setbacks in life.

When she was older, she discovered the same moral in a poem by Jessie Rittenhouse, *Windows,* which she committed to memory:

I looked through others' windows
On an enchanted earth,
But out of my own window —
Solitude and dearth.

And yet there is a mystery
I cannot understand —
That others through my window
See an enchanted land.

On her sixteenth birthday (Orv's nineteenth), Katie cried because the family was getting old. Everyone, it seemed, was growing up too fast. Her brothers had long since started supporting themselves. Orv had dropped out of high school and plunged full-time into a small printing operation. Soon Will joined him. Both had been good students but would never continue their studies. With the cycling craze of the 1890s, they expanded into bicycle sales, manufacture, and repair, and they hired Lorin to help out in the print shop. He had a wife and young son and desperately needed the work. Reuch, too, was struggling in Kansas City, Missouri, where he worked as a bookkeeper to support his wife and two small children.

Meanwhile, Katie had taken Susan's place as the light of the home. She cooked, cleaned, corresponded with absent family members, kept accounts, and served as her father's secretary — all while attending school. Milton had made it clear that she was to take care of him always. But he also wanted her to be independent after his death, so he did something very unusual for a father in those days: he sent his daughter to college.

Oberlin

I N SEPTEMBER 1893, Katharine boarded a train in Dayton for Oberlin College, a half-day away in a pretty town near the big industrial city of Cleveland. She chose this grown-up moment to start using her grown-up name. Hereafter, Katie would be Katharine to all except her family and childhood friends.

A year earlier she had been in Kansas City, helping Reuch's wife, Lou, get ready for her new baby. The very day Katharine returned to Dayton, Wilbur fell ill with appendicitis. Then a week later Lorin's wife, Netta, delivered her new baby. Between caring for the babies, the brother, and the bishop, Katharine hardly had time to get sick herself, which she did that winter with severe tonsillitis. As a result, she never graduated from high school, and Oberlin required her to spend a year in its preparatory program to get ready for the rigors of college work.

Few people attended college in the 1890s, and most who did were men. But there was a growing opinion in the United States that women, too, deserved the benefits of higher education. Some people felt that women should be educated at their own colleges. Others argued that women ought to

Oberlin College, 1905.

attend the same schools as men, in an arrangement called coeducation. Oberlin was the oldest coeducational college in the country. Unlike many such institutions, it didn't segregate men and women into different academic programs. Everyone at Oberlin got the same education — in Latin, Greek, mathematics, English literature, philosophy, history, science, and ethics. Graduates were well prepared for further training in a profession such as medicine or law, or they could go directly into teaching, which is what Bishop Wright had in mind for Katharine. Very few women entered a profession in those days. Teaching and nursing were about the only careers open to them.

In Milton's eyes, Oberlin was an ideal environment for his daughter. Tobacco and alcohol were forbidden; students rose at six o'clock and retired at ten; they attended daily prayers and wrote weekly reports on their moral conduct; and they attended special lectures by distinguished visitors. While Katharine was at Oberlin, Professor Woodrow Wilson of Princeton University came to lecture on democracy. Years later he would be elected president of the United States. Jane Addams came to talk about her remarkable community center for poor people in Chicago. Later she worked for women's rights and world disarmament and won a Nobel Peace Prize.

Oberlin knew how to foster excellence among its students too. In 1889 a young man named Robert Millikan was asked by his Greek professor to teach physics in the preparatory program. Millikan protested that he didn't know

Katharine (left) with Margaret Goodwin during their Oberlin years.

any physics. The professor insisted, "Anyone who can do well in my Greek can teach physics!" Millikan taught himself the subject over the summer and found his life's work in the process. He would later win a Nobel Prize for his research on atoms.

But college was not just prayer, study, and lectures. For the first time in her life, Katharine had sisters — or the next best thing. From a house full of men on Hawthorn Street she moved into a house full of women. Each school year she rented a room for a few dollars a week at one of the private boarding-houses for female students. Her roommates became her best friends for life. One was Margaret Goodwin, a minister's daughter from Chicago. Margaret and Katharine were so in love with campus life that they occasionally went astray — as during freshman year, when they sometimes neglected their studies to go ice-skating on the new college rink.

"Margaret was such good company always — never a bore," Katharine remembered much later. Once, when a teacher asked Margaret how she and Katharine always had so much to talk about together, Margaret replied that they just covered the same subjects over and over without realizing it.

They both belonged to L.L.S., which originally stood for Ladies' Literary Society. The name sounded stuffy to Katharine's generation, so they changed it to a Latin phrase with the same initials, *Litterae Laborum Solamen,* which translated: "literature is a solace from troubles." Club gatherings were devoted to different forms of public speaking. One was parliamentary practice, in which the president drilled members in the rules of motions, amendments, points of order, and other intricacies of running an orderly meeting.

Another club drill was extemporaneous speaking, which required members to discuss a subject without prior preparation. Once, Margaret was asked to talk about peace. "At first there was a frown and a look of dismay on Miss Goodwin's face," say the records, "then a vacant expression followed by a smile, which finally developed into a giggle. Having thus relieved herself, the ideas came readily and she discoursed at some length on peace, among nations, parties, and individuals."

On a different occasion the society teamed up with another women's club to hold an elaborate mock session of the U.S. House of Representatives, in which the issues of the day were debated and resolved with authentic parliamentary tactics.

If Katharine and Margaret were known for an excess of exuberance, then their friends Harriet Silliman and Kate Leonard made up for it with a surfeit of sobriety. Harriet, who shared a room with Katharine and Margaret, was serious and studious. Kate, who lived at home, was selfless and noble. Kate's parents were retired foreign missionaries who had settled in the town of Oberlin. Though by far the most pious of the four friends, Kate was an expert at winning arguments. During the same L.L.S. meeting at which Margaret discoursed on peace, Kate triumphed in a debate on deception. She was assigned to argue that deception is sometimes justified. She won by citing examples — probably of the "white-lie" variety — from her own experience.

Only women lived in Katharine's boardinghouse, but some men took their meals there. One was Henry J. Haskell, called Harry. He was also from

L.L.S., Katharine's literary club at Oberlin, 1897. "Weren't we funny with those top knots," she wrote three decades later.

Katharine is in the second vertical column, center.
Kate Leonard is in the second column, top.
Margaret Goodwin is in the third column, center.
Harriet Silliman is in the last column, center.

Harry Haskell (right) and his roommate in their Oberlin boardinghouse, about 1895.

a missionary family and had spent his early adolescence in Bulgaria, in what was then the Ottoman Empire, where his parents had founded a college. He was studious by nature and had spent much of his time reading books while growing up. As a result, he was two years ahead of Katharine at Oberlin, even though they were the same age.

Katharine appreciated Harry for the same qualities she admired in her women friends: kindness, nobility, and intelligence. He was brilliant in mathematics and helped her with freshman math review, a course required of all freshmen. During these sessions, which were held three times a week after breakfast, he was so intent on the problems that she had trouble telling if he actually liked her. But little by little, they became close friends.

Harry looked younger than his years, but he had grown-up opinions. He believed in reforming college regulations to give students more responsibility; he felt that Oberlin's "Ladies' Rules" governing hours and conduct of female students were unduly strict; and he spoke expertly about national politics and world events. This serious streak was lightened by a love for romantic short stories. He not only read them, he wrote them, and his success at selling several to national publications led him to plan a career as a short story writer after graduation.

During his senior year Harry fell in love with, and proposed to, one of Katharine's housemates, a joyous, energetic woman named Isabel Cummings, who was three years younger than Harry. She accepted under the then-usual terms that the wedding would be put off until the groom was established in a job. Such engagements could last years before the condition was met.

Engagements were definitely in the air during senior year. Young people on the verge of adult responsibilities made their first thrilling decisions about life. The wedding might be delayed, but courtship itself proceeded swiftly. Serious dating usually started in junior year, when couples began pairing off. The 1896 yearbook had this comment on the ritual: "There has commenced to exist between boys and girls a mild toleration of each other that has never before been apparent. It has become very common for them to bow to each other on the street, and at some of the socials a few of the bolder youths have even gone so far in their giddiness as to see Nellie home."

"Seeing Nellie Home" was a popular song of the day about a young man who proposes marriage while escorting his sweetheart home from a quilting party. Many engagements started in just this way.

Katharine, too, was swept up by romance. In 1896, while only a sophomore, she accepted the proposal of senior Arthur Cunningham — an earnest young scholar who played football and was captain of the baseball team. The following year, he went off to medical school in nearby Cleveland.

The engagement was still on when Katharine was a senior two years later. But she suspected that Arthur didn't really love her. "He didn't do anything wrong," she remembered three decades later, "but he was evidently relieved when I pretended I thought we had better give it up. I was horribly unhappy for several years, all the time glad I had done what I had but broken-hearted over the failure of a great ideal with me."

Oberlin class of 1896 football team.
Arthur Cunningham, Katharine's fiancé, is in the middle row, second from left.

She convinced herself that she had done the right thing, for afterward she referred to the broken engagement as "my narrow escape." Nor was she alone in being without romantic prospects. A group of fellow females, including Margaret and Harriet, took to calling themselves The Order of the Empty Heart, apparently in reference to their unengaged status.

Milton knew nothing about his daughter's wedding plans, and it's hard to say how he would have reacted. After all, he had not sent her to Oberlin to find a husband but to get an education. On that score he had no cause for complaint. Katharine excelled in her studies — particularly in Latin, Greek, English, and history. She even won a prestigious history prize and twenty-five dollars for an essay on the foreign policy of President James Monroe.

Oberlin gave her something else besides. Before she went away to college, her family had been her life. Now she had ties beyond the family — to her new friends and to the college itself.

"The Order of the Empty Heart" ready for an outing at Oberlin, about 1898.
Katharine is second from right. Margaret is third from right. Harriet is at far left.

One friend, it's true, had broken her heart. But scores of others would sustain her for a lifetime with happy memories of boardinghouses, skating parties, club meetings, bike rides, picnics, and sing-alongs, not to mention weird valentines, engrossing lectures, Harry's math help, and the lighthearted fellowship of The Order of the Empty Heart.

Struggling

KATHARINE GRADUATED FROM OBERLIN on June 22, 1898. She was twenty-three years old and armed with excellent job recommendations. Her professors praised her as a fine scholar, a promising teacher, and—although they didn't realize they were all using the same word—a "vivacious" person.

It did no good, at least not at first. On June 24, Dayton's school board

Katharine in her Oberlin graduation gown, 1898.

filled the new positions at Steele High School, and Katharine's name was not on the list.

Her friends Harriet and Kate were in the same boat. But Margaret was off and running. She had a teaching position in the small town of Canal Dover, Ohio. At fifty dollars a month she was earning even more than Harry Haskell, who had started at forty dollars a month two years earlier in his job as a cub reporter in Kansas City. Like many budding writers, he had had to give up his dream of penning short stories for a living.

A year later Katharine had her foot in the door as a part-time substitute at Steele, and Harriet and Kate had decided to go back to college to study music, increasing their chances of finding teaching jobs later.

Meanwhile, Wilbur was writing the Smithsonian for information about flight, and a few weeks later, when Margaret was visiting Katharine after their first Oberlin reunion, the packet of information came.

In this way, Katharine's teaching career was struggling off the ground at the same time her brothers were taking off in their new pursuit.

For several years the two efforts had separate but equal status around 7 Hawthorn Street. Katharine watched as her brothers grew more and more absorbed with the problem of flight, confident that they could make progress where others had failed. Without planning it, they were changing from printers and bicycle mechanics into expert aeronautical engineers. Katharine was fascinated, but she was too busy to participate. For their part, the brothers were curious about their sister's career. Wilbur was especially intrigued, since he had wanted to go to college and become a teacher himself. Orville, by contrast, was more attracted to Katharine's social life and friends. It was even rumored around the neighborhood that he was courting Agnes Osborn, a childhood friend of Katharine's who had planned to go to Oberlin but felt obliged to stay at home and take care of her grandmother. Nothing came of Orv's romance, and nothing came of Will's interest in teaching. Flight took over their lives to the exclusion of everything else.

Eventually flight came to dominate the lives of all the Wrights, ending Katharine's career in education and reconnecting her to Oberlin in a surprising way. But in 1899 that was all in the future.

Teaching

THE TURN OF THE NEW CENTURY brought Katharine a full-time teaching job at Steele. She immediately hired a housekeeper — fourteen-year-old Carrie Kayler, who would serve with the Wright family for the next half a century.

Steele High School was a brand-new five-story structure with magnificent archway entrances, imposing turrets, and a soaring bell tower. Forty teachers presided over twelve hundred students in its airy, if drafty, classrooms.

At the time, public high schools were just becoming widespread in America, and Steele prided itself on being second to none. Despite near universal enthusiasm for this new educational opportunity, dropout rates were high. Nationwide, less than half of those enrolled in high school ever graduated. None of the Wrights had high school diplomas, even though Reuch, Lorin, and Katharine went on to college — where Katharine was the only Wright to earn a degree.

On average, high school girls outnumbered boys by about three to two, and they graduated at an even higher rate. This caused considerable consternation among school administrators, who were mostly men. They theorized that the predominance of female teachers was driving boys away. It was "little short of monstrous," said one male official, that high school boys got "almost all of their intellectual and moral impulse from female teachers."

Another authority, also male, expressed similar amazement that girls were up to the challenge of high school. He warned of the terrible price they would pay for straining their brains over books, only to "stagger through the ceremonies of diploma-giving to return to their homes condemned to invalidism for life."

Even if girls were getting most of the degrees, finishing high school was still considered prestigious. And the most prestigious graduates were those who specialized in Katharine's field: Latin and Greek. These ancient languages were regarded as refined, precise, and expressive tools of the mind whose mastery required mental discipline that molded character.

The Wrights at play.

Above: While Milton is out of town in September 1899, Katharine and Orville host a party. In the front row, Katharine is at far right, next to Margaret; Orville is at far left. Harriet is in the back row, second from left.

Right: Another party in September 1899. The leaves and Japanese lantern hanging from the chandelier commemorate a recent camping trip taken by most of those present. Katharine is at left, with her back to the camera. Harriet is looking at a photograph. Margaret is second from right. Orville is standing.

Harriet and Katharine (right), probably during summer vacation, 1900. Harriet has just finished a year of music study at Oberlin, while Katharine is newly established as a full-time Latin teacher at Steele High School.

Above: Carrie Kaylor (right), housekeeper for the Wright family, dressed up for New Year's Eve, 1900.

Right: Katharine (back to camera) and Harriet in the living room at 7 Hawthorn Street, 1899.

Educators of the day made a distinction between "training" subjects and "information" subjects. The training subjects were Latin, Greek, and mathematics. These laid the groundwork for a lifetime of learning by exercising the mind just as an athlete exercises the muscles. Information subjects were history, science, and other fact-based disciplines.

According to authorities, information subjects were best acquired after the training subjects. Some experts even felt that information subjects had no place in school at all. For example, in 1896 President Charles W. Eliot of Harvard University declared before a crowded auditorium: "The less we know about the chemistry and biology of the air of this room, the more comfortably we shall breathe it. We can ride quite happily in an electric car without having the slightest conception of what electricity is." This attitude helps explain Wilbur's regret at never having mastered Latin and Greek, even though he and Orville could not have invented the airplane without a deep knowledge of information subjects such as physics and engineering.

Katharine's status as a novice teacher earned her the least desirable assignment in her department: beginning Latin. Since Latin was required of all students at Steele, Katharine was faced with quick learners and slow, hard workers and slackers, curious pupils and bored. Fortunately, she had a knack for dealing with mischievous boys, who were always a problem. "I had five or six notoriously bad boys assigned to my room," she wrote Milton in the fall of 1901. "I was ready for them and nipped their smartness in the bud." She didn't say how, but she probably picked up the technique from growing up with four older brothers.

As she grew in experience Katharine should have been given Greek classes to teach. Greek was taken by college-bound students, who needed a year or two of the language to satisfy most colleges' entrance requirements. Having already conquered the intricacies of Latin grammar, which was similar to Greek, these motivated scholars could move quickly into some of the pearls of ancient literature, such as Homer, Plato, and Euripides. Unfortunately, at Steele the head of Katharine's department reserved these interesting courses for himself. A relative newcomer — especially a woman — could not expect such an assignment, regardless of her experience or abilities.

The situation was somewhat similar to that faced by Will and Orv in the flight field. They, too, were newcomers faced with entrenched old-timers. Even though human flight was the most fascinating and difficult technical problem of the age, it was still dominated by uncreative minds stuck in unproductive ruts. But unlike Katharine, who had to answer to an overbearing boss, Wilbur and Orville had to answer to no one. They were free to take the expert advice or leave it. So they left it . . . far behind.

Learning

N O ONE KNOWS HOW LONG humans have dreamed of flying like birds. Many have had the dream, a few have tried to make it a reality, and a tiny fraction of those have achieved some progress toward the goal.

When the Wrights first set to work on the problem of flight in 1899, the world authority on the subject was a retired civil engineer in Chicago named Octave Chanute. Chanute's book, *Progress in Flying Machines*, covered every major idea for achieving winged flight since Leonardo da Vinci's flapping wing contraption from the late 1400s. With more and more thinkers applying themselves to the problem as the twentieth century approached, Chanute was confident that the solution was near.

He didn't know what a successful flying machine would look like, but he was sure that several recent developments pointed the way. One was that Samuel P. Langley, head of the Smithsonian Institution, had shown how wings produce lift. Another was that Hiram Maxim, inventor of a portable machine gun, had built a giant steam-powered airplane capable of uncontrolled flight a few inches off the ground. Yet another was that the German Otto Lilienthal had conducted gliding experiments showing that the most pressing problem was making airplanes automatically stable in unpredictable wind gusts. Unfortunately, one such gust killed Lilienthal in 1896.

Chanute's confidence that investigators were on the right track was widely shared. But Wilbur and Orville believed that he was wrong. They were suspicious of the way Langley had compiled his wing data. They thought that Maxim's machine was pointless if it could not be controlled. And they were convinced that the instability of an airplane in wind gusts didn't matter, as long as the pilot had an effective way to steer the craft—which Lilienthal had not.

Though they disagreed with Chanute's judgments, the brothers had great respect for his encyclopedic knowledge of all things pertaining to flight. So they introduced themselves by mail and asked his advice on several small matters, while keeping him informed of their research.

Chanute responded enthusiastically. In June 1901 he stopped by Dayton on a trip to Tennessee. Katharine presided as hostess at lunch. Planning the meal with her customary care, she selected fresh melon for dessert and instructed Carrie to pick a large, juicy piece for the guest. When Carrie cut the two melons that were available, she found that only one was ripe. Deciding that everyone at the table deserved a piece, she divided it evenly into small servings. Katharine was mortified, but Chanute was apparently unoffended, since soon he was more involved with Will and Orv than ever.

That summer he visited Kitty Hawk during the brothers' second season of gliding experiments. Will and Orv were concentrating on learning how to make a glider steer up, down, left, and right. In other words, they were learning to fly. Only after they had mastered this skill would they attack the problem of powering their craft. Practically everyone else in the field was doing it the other way around, on the theory that they would learn how to steer an airplane once they got it off the ground.

Chanute was so impressed with the brothers' approach that he invited Wilbur to give a speech at the fall meeting of the Western Society of Engineers in Chicago. He naturally assumed that Wilbur was the senior member of the Wright team. Not only was he older and more dignified than his dapper brother, but he also appeared to be the more profound thinker. Whether or not this was true, Orville abhorred speaking in public and was happy to defer on all occasions to his partner.

Nonetheless, Wilbur was a little frightened to appear before Chanute's august group—until Katharine convinced him to do it. "Will was about to refuse but I nagged him into going," she wrote Milton. "He will get acquainted with some scientific men and it may do him a lot of good."

Will showed up wearing Orv's fancy shirt, collar, and cuff links, which considerably enhanced his own slightly shabby suit. He proceeded to deliver a well-organized, thoughtful address, giving this memorable description of the Wright approach to the problem of flight: "There are two ways of learning how to ride a fractious horse: one is to get on him and learn by actual practice how each motion and trick may be best met; the other is to sit on a fence and watch the beast a while, and then retire to the house and at leisure figure out the best way of overcoming his jumps and kicks. The latter system is the safest, but the former, on the whole, turns out the larger proportion of good riders. It is very much the same in learning to ride a flying machine."

Riding a flying machine, Wilbur explained, was far from simple. Most experimenters assumed that left and right turns would be made with a vertical rudder, like a ship's. Turning the rudder left, for example, would turn the craft left. Or so it was thought. The Wrights were convinced that this was incorrect. They believed that in order to turn, an airplane had to bank—or roll—just as a cyclist does by leaning into a turn. The same mechanism used for banking would also keep the craft balanced side-to-side in rough air, solving part of the problem that had plagued Lilienthal.

As their experiments progressed, the brothers found that riding a flying machine was even more complicated than this. They eventually learned that a smooth turn required two actions: they had to roll the plane, which they did by warping the wings to produce higher lift on one side than the other; and they had to yaw, or point, the craft left or right into the direction of the turn, which they achieved with a vertical rudder. Completing their controls was a horizontal rudder to pitch the machine up or down, seesaw fashion, providing a way to keep the craft balanced front-to-back.

As if control problems weren't enough, Will and Orv discovered that they had to reinvent the wing. Langley and Lilienthal had compiled extensive tables that showed the amount of lifting force produced by wings with different shapes moving at different speeds and angles through the air. But Will and

Orv learned by hard experience that this information was not reliable. As with so much else in their work on the airplane, they had to start from scratch —first to understand and then to solve this crucial piece of the puzzle.

Kitty Hawk

K ATHARINE WATCHED her brothers' learning adventure with a mixture of interest and mock irritation. "We don't hear anything but flying machine . . . from morning till night. I'll be glad when school begins so I can escape," she wrote Milton in September 1901, just before Wilbur's Chicago speech.

A year later she sounded a note of melancholy as the boys labored over the cloth covering for their wings: "The flying machine is in process of making now. Will spins the sewing machine around by the hour while Orv squats around marking the places to sew. There is no place in the house to live but I'll be lonesome enough by this time next week and wish that I could have some of their racket around."

Despite Katharine's proximity to the manufacturing process, she would have to wait several years before seeing what her brothers were actually doing. Until then, her only picture of their experiments came in letters from Kitty Hawk. Most were written by Orv, and most concerned the humor and minutiae of life on the Carolina coast, with hardly a mention of the excitement and challenge of trying to fly like a bird.

When members of the Wright family wrote to each other, they seldom spoke of their hopes, fears, and enthusiasms. Instead, they tried to describe what it was like to be wherever they happened to be. For instance, Katharine learned all about Bill Tate, "postmaster, farmer, fisherman, and political boss of Kitty Hawk," as Orv described him—who owned one of the finest houses in the area, an unpainted, rough-hewn, two-story affair, without rugs, books, pictures, and with hardly any furniture. Not that the Tate family felt any privation, noted Orv, since no one in Kitty Hawk had very much to start with.

Bill Tate and family at their Kitty Hawk home, where they hosted the Wright brothers in 1900. Like many Wright photos, this one was damaged in a flood that inundated Dayton in 1913.

Orv also related how his and Will's arrival at Kitty Hawk in September 1900 precipitated a food shortage: "We, having more money than the natives, have been able to buy up the whole egg product of the town and about all the canned goods in the store. I fear some of them will have to suffer as a result."

Even so, the natives were more than grateful for the company. Strangers rarely came to Kitty Hawk, and word quickly spread about the birdmen from Dayton. The fact that they were brothers was a convenience, since it made it safe to address any unfamiliar male face as "Mr. Wright."

Messrs. Wright lived with the Tates at first; then, they camped out in a tent pitched on the windswept dunes. Eventually, they built a shed for their glider and another for their residence. They were seldom alone. Mosquitoes, bedbugs, mice, and wild pigs tormented them at various times — sometimes all at once. In the evenings, while not fighting varmints, Orv studied French for fun and Will wrote up the day's flight tests, if there had been any.

Above, left: Wilbur and Orville test their 1901 glider as a kite at Kitty Hawk.
Above, right: The 1902 glider gives better results, thanks to an improved wing shape that produces more lift.

They didn't represent their activities as anything but a vacation. "I look upon it as a pleasure trip pure and simple," Will wrote his father in 1900. Two years later Orv described their loafing life in a letter to Katharine: "We have three regular occupations now, with occasionally a fourth — eating, sleeping, chasing pigs and mice, and gliding now and then when the weather is favorable and the machine is not in the repair shop."

In fact, they were being deceptive about their motive, for they were as ambitious in their fun as Katharine had been in her studies at Oberlin. Like her, they were engaged in pleasurable preparation for a new career.

In his Chicago speech, Wilbur had stated that when proper balance and steering could be demonstrated, "the age of flying machines will have arrived, for all other difficulties are of minor importance." That was not entirely true, for when the brothers had mastered the art of control, perfected their wing, and were ready to hitch a motor and propellers to their glider, they discovered that they faced still more problems.

They had always assumed that designing an airplane propeller would be

Above, left: The fully controllable 1902 glider paves the way for a powered flyer.
Above, right: Four successful powered flights on December 17, 1903, end with a broken front rudder.

easy, based on the mathematical theory of ship propellers. But no such theoretical work existed, so they had to do the calculations themselves. And when they wrote to automobile manufacturers for help with a lightweight internal combustion engine, they discovered that here, again, they were on their own.

On December 17, 1903, all the problems seemed solved as the brothers took turns making four powered takeoffs over the dunes at Kitty Hawk. History records these as the first controlled, sustained, powered flights of an airplane. But had the brothers really produced a successful flying machine? According to their own standards, probably not. All four takeoffs ended with an uncontrolled dive into the sand. And the last plunge broke the horizontal rudder, putting the machine out of commission.

This was not exactly the goal aimed at by generations of dreamers gazing up at the effortless flight of birds. But it was a start.

PART THREE ❧ *The Journey*

The Fair

IN JUNE 1904, six months after Will and Orv's powered flights at Kitty Hawk, Katharine traveled to the World's Fair in St. Louis to spend several weeks with Margaret, who was now Mrs. Cola W. Meacham. After teaching at Canal Dover for a year, Margaret had moved to small-town schools in Illinois and Minnesota before marrying Mr. Meacham on New Year's Eve, 1901.

The couple lived in Margaret's beloved hometown of Chicago. There, Mr. Meacham was a businessman and Margaret was a secretary for a teacher placement agency. Margaret's father, Reverend Goodwin, had died a few years earlier. Soon after, her mother was evicted from the retirement house supplied by Reverend Goodwin's church, where he had preached for over thirty years. This dire situation probably hastened Margaret's marriage, so she could afford to take care of her mother.

Katharine and Margaret were meeting at the most exciting vacation spot in America—the lavish exposition celebrating the centennial of the Louisiana Purchase. One hundred years earlier the United States had bought Louisiana Territory from France. From 1804 to 1806 captains Meriwether Lewis and William Clark explored this vast wilderness, which extended from the Mississippi River to the crest of the Rocky Mountains. They traveled by foot and boat. Barely a century later the same ground would be covered by railroads linking farms, ranches, towns, and cities that had been empty patches of prairie when the explorers passed through.

Previous pages:
Katharine (center) and a friend go for a ride with Orville, early 1900s.

The St. Louis Exposition, 1904. Ahead are gardens leading to the U.S. Government Building. The Palace of Liberal Arts is on the left; Mines and Metallurgy is on the right.

This remarkable change in America was one of the themes of the exposition, which had palaces of Transportation, Electricity, Mines and Metallurgy, Machinery, Manufacturers, and Varied Industries—all displaying the latest advances of a civilization confident that it faced no limits on what it could accomplish.

Katharine and Margaret dutifully sampled these technological showcases. "We walked through the Transportation and Machinery buildings and through one corner of the Varied Industries. Mr. Meacham is in Machinery Hall," Katharine informed her father. But the two women were probably more attracted to the palaces of Fine Arts and Liberal Arts, by the beautiful lakes and gardens, and by the many cultural exhibits that featured people from faraway lands. They could sample German, Italian, and other foreign foods, along with several new dishes developed especially for the fair: iced tea, ice-cream cones, hot dogs, and a spun-sugar confection called "fairy floss," later known as cotton candy.

Very likely one of these delicacies was blamed when Margaret fell ill with intestinal trouble in July. Katharine stayed in St. Louis as doctors tried to diagnose the illness but couldn't. Eventually, Margaret began to recover and Katharine returned to Dayton, where Milton immediately put her to work writing letters to his church correspondents.

Wilbur and Orville also planned a trip to the fair — not for pleasure, but to enter their flying machine in a competition arranged in part by Octave Chanute. In January 1904, Chanute had come to Dayton to congratulate the brothers on their successful powered flights at Kitty Hawk and to urge them to show off their machine at the St. Louis Exposition. Ever optimistic about the progress of the flying art, Chanute believed that the Wright airplane was capable of winning a $100,000 grand prize offered at the fair for three flights over a 10-mile course. So far, the flyer had flown no farther than 852 feet — about one sixtieth of the needed distance.

Certainly, no other winged vehicle in existence could compete with the Wright flyer. However, the committee setting the rules didn't distinguish between airplanes and powered balloons, known as airships. Balloons had been covering long distances for over a century, while airplanes were in their infancy. A competition that included both was like a race between a locomotive and a bicycle.

Even so, the Wrights believed they had a chance. In January they started work on a sturdier machine with a modified wing shape and a more powerful engine. They also started scouting for a more convenient test site. Kitty Hawk was just too far from Dayton if their flight hobby was to become something more than an annual vacation from the Wright Cycle Company. Besides, a truly practical flyer had to operate anywhere — not just in the helpful winds and cushioning dunes of Kitty Hawk.

They soon found a promising spot 8 miles from Dayton on a trolley line. A large field called Huffman Prairie was offered by the owner free of charge as long as the brothers promised to shoo away grazing cows before their experiments. By mid-May they had completed a work shed on the site and put the finishing touches on a new flyer.

They invited the press to a demonstration flight on May 23. About a

Orville (left) and Wilbur at Huffman Prairie outside Dayton,
about the time of their failed demonstration flight for the press, May 1904.

dozen reporters came, along with Milton, Lorin and his family, and numerous neighbors and friends. Katharine couldn't make it, since she had to teach. Unfortunately, nothing went right. At first there was too much wind. Then there was too little. The brothers needed at least some wind to take off, but too much was dangerous.

They waited. The air stayed calm. Then they announced they would start the engine and run the machine down the launch rail. Maybe it would take off; maybe it wouldn't. At least reporters would see what was involved.

With the engine misfiring badly, the flyer rolled down the track and off the end without rising an inch. Reporters felt cheated. Will and Orv invited them back the next day for another attempt. But almost all stayed away, certain that the age of flying machines had not yet arrived.

In the following week, more setbacks convinced the brothers that there was no future in trying to influence how newspapers reported their work. So they decided to dispense with publicity — which was a good thing, since that spring and summer were full of false starts, crashes, and baffling problems. Even with the improvements over their 1903 flyer, the 1904 machine was still barely able to get off the ground. A balky engine, a broken propeller, not enough wind, too much wind, an unusually hot day, or some other difficulty usually kept their machine firmly earthbound.

But sometimes it did fly. On August 23, Katharine was present as first Orville and then Wilbur took to the air for less than a minute each. It was the first time she had ever seen them aloft. Nothing prepared her for the sight of the wobbly contraption lurching down its launch rail like a rickety cart going downhill, bumping up and down, up and down, then suddenly up . . . up! . . . up! — as if being pulled into the air by invisible wires. It was magical!

Within a month Will and Orv were making complete circles around Huffman Prairie. But they were still in no shape to compete at St. Louis. On the other hand, neither was anyone else. Not even an airship could finish the course that year — which was just as well, for the fair was broke and could not have paid the winner anyway, despite all the earnings from iced tea, ice-cream cones, hot dogs, and fairy floss.

Curiosity

LONG AFTER THE EVENTS described in this book, the head of a charitable organization in New York City came to Ohio to give a speech. Charlotte Carr had grown up in Dayton and wanted to use an incident from her youth to show how skepticism can sometimes be taken too far. She described how forty-four years earlier she had been sitting in her high school Latin class when the teacher made a surprising announcement:

Opposite: This impressive flight at Huffman Prairie
was witnessed by Katharine and Milton on October 5, 1905.
Gradually the brothers were refining their invention into a practical flying machine.

"Anyone who would like to see a flying machine should go out to Huffman Prairie this afternoon."

No one went, since no one believed such a thing was possible.

The teacher was Katharine Wright. She also invited fellow teachers to witness this new wonder, but they stayed away too.

Charlotte Carr urged her listeners to wake up and take notice when opportunity knocked—even if it came in such outlandish guise as a flying machine. After all, it just might work.

Because Huffman Prairie was on a trolley line, some people eventually did see the flying machine, quite by accident. Puzzled by the sight of a giant motor-powered kite buzzing around with a man aboard, a few of these witnesses approached the local newspapers. "Did you know about this?" they asked. Newsmen were in no mood to hear about the Wrights after the failed demonstration flight of May 23. Even reporters who believed the witnesses assumed that whatever the brothers were doing couldn't possibly be important.

"I sort of felt sorry for them," recalled Luther Beard of the _Dayton Journal_. "They seemed like well-meaning, decent enough young men. Yet here they were, neglecting their business to waste their time day after day on that ridiculous flying machine. I had an idea that it must worry their father."

But just in case, Beard asked Orv to let him know if he and Will ever did anything newsworthy. Happy to avoid publicity for the time being, Orv downplayed their progress.

"Done anything of special interest lately?" Beard asked Orv one day.

"Oh, nothing much," said Orv. "Today one of us flew for nearly five minutes."

Beard concluded that if the inventor himself thought it was "nothing much," then it must not be worth reporting.

Ignored by the press, Will and Orv could focus calmly on the problems of their new technology. In the fall of 1904 they started using a catapult launch system. This device propelled the machine down its track by means of a rope attached to a heavy weight, which was dropped from a small tower. With it they were no longer at the mercy of the wind for takeoff, and by the end of the year they had amassed a total of forty-five minutes in the air.

The next year they built a new flyer and were airborne so often that local farmers got bored with the sight. One man cutting corn spied the machine aloft and said to his helper, "Well, the boys are at it again." The two men kept working until they got to the end of the row. "The durned thing was still going round," the farmer recalled. "I thought it never *would* stop." It finally did — after thirty-nine minutes and more than 24 miles circling around and around Huffman Prairie.

Dayton citizens got so used to the flying machine that it didn't seem like news, even if the rest of America was still oblivious to it. But in Europe flight enthusiasts *had* heard of the Wrights — thanks to the efforts of Chanute, who was a native of France and had many friends abroad. Across the Atlantic, people were curious — very curious — about these mysterious brothers.

Grief

MARGARET NEVER FULLY RECOVERED after she fell ill at the St. Louis fair. A few months later, in spring 1905, the symptoms returned. Doctors suspected tuberculosis, the same bacterial infection that had killed Susan Wright in 1889. In Margaret's case the disease did not show up in her lungs but in her intestines, and it was probably contracted from contaminated milk. A year later it spread to her brain. On May 3, 1906, the exuberant young woman who had been Katharine's sister in spirit at Oberlin died in agony. She was a few days short of her thirtieth birthday.

In the following months, Katharine got more and more involved in her brothers' work. Everyone else in the family was busy. Milton had his church. Lorin had his family. Reuch was farming in another state. But since Margaret's death Katharine was emotionally adrift. The airplane was something to take her mind off her grief, something she could watch with pride — and worry — as it grew, something she could roll up her sleeves and take part in.

At this point, Will and Orv had stopped flight-testing and were trying to sell their invention, which was proving far more difficult than they expected.

The U.S. Army was strangely indifferent to owning a machine that the brothers believed would revolutionize warfare by making surprise attacks impossible. The Barnum and Bailey Circus was briefly interested, but nothing came of it. Only European governments were truly enthusiastic about acquiring an airplane.

Perhaps this was because Europeans were starting to see public demonstrations of flying machines. On October 23, 1906, a ramshackle plane, guided by a Brazilian airship pilot named Alberto Santos-Dumont, made a powered hop of about 200 feet in a park in Paris. Three weeks later Santos-Dumont flew 700 feet, or nearly as far as the Wrights' longest flight at Kitty Hawk on December 17, 1903.

Although Santos-Dumont had almost no control over his craft and it invariably fell to pieces on landing, his feats were hailed as the dawn of a new era. Many regarded him as the first person ever to fly, since there was widespread debate about whether the Wrights had really flown.

Europeans didn't know what to make of the brothers. If their flights had actually taken place, asked the skeptics, why weren't the Wrights getting more attention in the American press, which was famous for being the most aggressive in the world? Of course, in America the press either didn't believe the brothers were flying, or, like Luther Beard, they didn't believe it was unusual to do so. In a sense, Wilbur and Orville were so far ahead of the competition that they were invisible.

They were ahead because they had paid attention to the problem that was just now becoming evident to their rivals: an airplane is useless unless it can be controlled. But the brothers knew that when others saw how they maneuvered by coordinating roll, yaw, and pitch, the cat would be out of the bag. Therefore they applied for patents to get legal protection over their discoveries. Once patents were issued, they would be able to make money either by selling airplanes outright or by licensing others to manufacture them.

As they got deeper and deeper into the details of turning their invention into a business, Wilbur and Orville were changing from carefree inventors into nervous businessmen. In May 1907, Wilbur sailed for Europe to try to negotiate airplane deals. Orville joined him in July. Naturally the interested governments wanted to see a flight first. But the brothers wanted a contract first, insisting that if their machine met certain performance goals for speed, altitude, duration, and maneuverability, then they expected to be paid. Otherwise, they would be giving away their secrets for free. This reluctance to show what they could do made them look suspiciously like bluffers — *les bluffeurs,* the French called them.

Oddly enough, as soon as the brothers went to Europe because no one in America was interested in their machine, people in America got *very* interested. This gave Katharine something to do. Every day she taught school until early afternoon. Then she came home and took care of airplane business. A wealthy flight enthusiast in Boston wanted three copies of a Wright pamphlet; she sent them. *Webster's Dictionary* wanted to publish a photograph of a Wright glider; she wrote Will and Orv asking if they had objections. Newspapermen called about sensational rumors concerning the brothers; she set the reporters straight. Visitors arrived with business offers, always more favorable to themselves than to the Wrights; she was courteous but noncommittal. Cranks wrote with their own peculiar propositions; she wrote back, politely declining.

Milton hardly noticed that Katharine had turned into a secretary for her brothers. In his eyes she had only one other occupation besides teaching: her social life. "She throws herself into the excitement of company, not forgetting to do her full share of the conversation in an excited manner," he complained to Wilbur.

Katharine complained back: "Every peculiarity that Pop ever had is in full blossom now. I can't leave home even in the daytime without being lectured. . . . It is a pathetic state of affairs when going for the cream is treasured up as the chief diversion of the evening!" She exaggerated slightly. Many of her letters describe charming gatherings with high school colleagues — a turkey dinner, an engagement celebration, a bridge game, a Halloween party featuring costumes and a fortune-teller.

At the last event, Katharine's fortune reflected the new aura of celebrity that was beginning to attach to the Wright family:

You'll early leave this earthly sphere,
But not by death! Oh! No!
You'll guide an airship without fear,
Win fame and a rich beau.

But tragedy soon touched her life again. Shortly after the Halloween party, Frances Mathews, a fellow Latin teacher who had recently resigned to get married, had a relapse in her long struggle with tuberculosis. Two weeks later she died.

Frances and Katharine used to take long walks in the country two or three times a week after school. Frances was under doctor's orders to get fresh air. Katharine went to keep her company. Sometimes they would cover as many as 15 miles. During these hikes they learned the trick of recognizing trees without their leaves.

"They are so interesting," Katharine wrote many years later of bare trees and the lessons learned during these outings with Frances, "some so graceful, some so sturdy, some with such beautiful black bark, others with such very lacy branches. . . . I never come in our entrance on a winter day that I don't notice the trees outlined against the sky on the west. Of course they are finest in the evening."

Fame

BY EARLY 1908 the brothers had two contracts and were ready to start demonstration flights. One agreement was with a French company, and in May, Wilbur boarded an ocean liner for his second trip abroad. The other contract was with the U.S. Army, which had changed its mind and was now interested in owning a flying machine. Orville was responsible for the army tests, which were scheduled for late summer at Fort Myer, Virginia, near Washington, D.C.

The brothers had built several copies of their latest flyer, which incorporated many improvements. Most noticeable was that the pilot now sat in a seat, instead of lying prone, and next to him was a seat for a passenger.

Although the Wrights were making headway selling airplanes, others were beginning to break into the field. After the halting hops made by Santos-Dumont in 1906, more airmen had gone aloft. In 1907 several pilots in France made straight-line flights lasting up to seventy-four seconds. In January 1908 a pilot named Henri Farman thrilled the world by guiding a dangerously out-of-control machine on a wavering circle of about a mile, winning a $10,000 prize. Also in 1908, an American motorcycle daredevil named Glenn Curtiss covered just over a mile in his plane *June Bug* and won a magnificent silver trophy.

The Wrights had been performing far more impressive feats since 1904. But instead of prize judges and journalists, their witnesses had been farmers, trolley passengers, friends, and a few cows.

This was about to change. On August 8, 1908, Wilbur started demonstration flights at a racetrack in Le Mans, France. He began with two quick circuits of the field. Spectators reacted as if seeing Aladdin unroll a carpet and execute aerial acrobatics. They went wild with excitement — for such was the difference between Wilbur's exquisitely controlled maneuvers and the awkward leaps of Santos-Dumont, Farman, and the rest. The Wrights were *bluffeurs* no more.

"The spectacle was marvelous and delightful," wrote a French witness. "We beheld the great white bird soar above the race course. . . . We were able to follow easily each movement of the pilot, note his extraordinary proficiency in the flying business, perceive the curious warping of the wings. . . . To behold this flying machine turn sharp round at the end of the wood at a height of 60 feet, and continue on its course, is an enchanting spectacle. . . . In a word, the Wright brothers are the first men who have succeeded in imitating birds. To deny it would be childish."

What no one realized was that Wilbur was only checking out his machine in preparation for some *real* flying. By the end of the year, he had made over a hundred takeoffs in France, dazzling tens of thousands of spectators with fancy figure eights, ascents to altitudes approaching 400 feet, and marathon flights lasting over two hours and covering almost 80 miles. He carried aloft sixty passengers, including student pilots who were learning the ropes on machines being bought under the French contract. Wilbur earned the nickname *l'homme-oiseau*, the birdman, and became an overnight celebrity.

Such success abroad should have prepared Americans for Orville's equally stunning flights at Fort Myer. But again, spectators reacted as if seeing something totally unexpected.

Indeed, over the next generation, people everywhere had the same response on witnessing their first airplane in action: they were shocked. As Orville explained to a journalist in 1925: "You ask why it was that the public took so little notice of our 1903 flights and not until 1908 awoke to the fact that human flight had actually been accomplished. I think it was mainly due to the fact that human flight was generally looked upon as an impossibility, and that scarcely any one believed in it until he actually saw it with his own eyes."

Back in Dayton, Katharine and Milton were taking the newfound family fame in stride. The previous year Katharine had been most interested in her brothers' reaction to Europe's cultural riches. "Take a good squint at Westminster and the British Museum. See the mummies and the old Latin manuscripts for me," she wrote Will when he was passing through London in May 1907. Now she was fascinated by the trappings of their sudden celebrity. "Suppose you tell me a few things when you write!" she scolded him on August 27, 1908, during his first month of flights. "What do I care about the position of the trees on the practice ground? Hey! Hey! Sterchens wants to hear all about the beautiful young ladies and the flowers and champagne!"

Which was exactly what Milton did *not* want to hear about. "I hope you will not dishonor the training I have given you on Sabbath, temperance etc.," he wrote in a typical fatherly sermon. "They are such as the best element of the American people approve, and it is to your interest, as well as those of the morality of America (and France) that you honor them."

On the subject of fame he had this warning: "Indeed they treat you in France as if you were a resurrected Columbus; and the people gaze as if you had fallen down from Jupiter. Enjoy fame ere its decadence, for I have realized the emptiness of its trumpet blasts."

Falling

ATHARINE DIDN'T HAVE TIME to dwell on fame's trumpet blasts, since Lorin's son Milton was sick with typhoid fever. The disease developed in the summer of 1908, when Wilbur was making his first flights in France. The fifteen-year-old was briefly near death; then he pulled through and had a long recovery, attended by his mother and aunt Katharine.

Typhoid fever was a much-feared intestinal disease common in cities and spread by poor sanitation. About one eighth of all victims died. Orville himself had survived a bout with the illness in 1896. Ever after, the Wrights had been scrupulous about the source of their drinking water. When away from home, they tried to get only water that had been boiled to kill bacteria.

While young Milton was on the mend and Orv was preparing for his Fort Myer flights, Katharine faced a distressing development in her career. Dayton had a new school superintendent who was bent on saving money by reducing the salaries of female teachers. It was a great blow that just when her brothers were riding high after their years without recognition, she was on the verge of being demoted.

But the biggest blow came on the evening of September 17, after Orville had been impressing crowds at Fort Myer for two weeks. Bishop Wright was out of town, and Katharine was at home alone when a telegram came:

FORT MYER, VA. SEPT. 17
ON FALLING WITH AEROPLANE AT FIVE THIRTY THIS AFTERNOON,
ORVILLE WRIGHT RECEIVED FRACTURE OF RIBS ON LEFT SIDE AND
FRACTURE OF THIGH CONDITION NOT CRITICAL. LIEUT. LAHM

Suspecting that Orv was more seriously injured than the telegram let on, Katharine quickly packed, called to arrange a substitute teacher, asked a friend to contact Bishop Wright as soon as he was awake the next morning, and barely an hour and a half after getting the news, she was on the ten o'clock train

Lieutenant Thomas Selfridge (bareheaded) sits in the flyer next to Orville before the disastrous flight at Fort Myer, Virginia, on September 17, 1908.

to Washington. She arrived the next afternoon. Lieutenant Lahm met her at the station, and they immediately drove to the army hospital at Fort Myer.

Lieutenant Frank P. Lahm had played a key role in getting the U.S. Army interested in the Wright flyer. An expert balloonist, in 1906 he had won the first International Balloon Race while assigned to cavalry school in France. The following year he was introduced to the Wright brothers during their first European trip. Lahm was recovering from typhoid at the time, but he was alert enough to recognize the military value of a flying machine. Later he prodded his superiors to arrange the Fort Myer tests, at which he himself was present. During the first week of flights Orville took him aloft for six circuits of the parade ground, which served as the flying field.

As he was driving Katharine to the hospital he described how his fellow officer Lieutenant Thomas Selfridge was sitting next to Orville on the ill-fated flight the previous day. Several minutes after takeoff, while Orv was

Lieutenant Frank P. Lahm (left) and Glenn Curtiss at Fort Myer, 1909.
Lahm became a lifelong friend of the Wrights. Curtiss, a prominent pilot and inventor,
would try to undermine the brothers' patent claims.

making his fourth circuit of the field, the machine suddenly shuddered, veered to one side, and plunged 75 feet to the ground. Lieutenant Selfridge was pinned beneath the wreckage. He died three hours later. The son of a prominent admiral, Selfridge had been a prestigious and enthusiastic student of the new technology. Now he had become its first victim.

Most witnesses assumed that Orville was as seriously injured as his passenger. But he was conscious as rescuers carried him away. Doctors found he had broken his left leg near the knee, fractured two or three ribs, and sustained severe scalp wounds. He was in bad shape, but they believed he would live.

When Katharine walked into Orv's hospital room, she saw his chin quiver and his eyes fill with tears. "Dear Little Brother!" she wrote later, using her most affectionate nickname for him. "He was so badly hurt. I never did anything much harder than walking into his room at the Hospital and smiling as if nothing much was the matter. He said afterward he thought it couldn't be so bad or I wouldn't have acted as I did."

She tried to cheer him up, but all he could think of was the accident. He was terribly upset about Selfridge and desperate to know what had gone wrong with the machine. Katharine stayed for twenty minutes. Then she left so he could get some sleep.

Privately the doctors had dreaded her coming and were surprised and relieved that she wasn't hysterical. They were even more relieved that she knew exactly what to do. Ever since her mother's illness, Katharine had been perfecting the art of caring for the sick.

For the next six weeks she gave her brother nearly constant attention. She spent all night, every night, at the hospital. She bathed him, read to him, received visitors, talked to his doctors, answered his mail, and often just sat silent in his room while he slept. She left around dawn each day to get breakfast and some sleep. Then she was back by mid-afternoon.

In the beginning she stayed with relatives of a Dayton friend. Then Lieutenant Lahm found her an inexpensive hotel nearby.

She promised her father that she would write every day, but some days she was just too tired. "It is now Saturday afternoon," Milton complained after a three-day gap in her correspondence. "The natural inference is that you are down with typhoid fever."

One night, while writing a letter to Wilbur, she broke down in the middle of a sentence. "I can't remember what I was going to say," she scribbled.

Wilbur was still making impressive flights in France, which cheered Orv considerably. It showed that the accident was due to a fluke rather than a design flaw in the machine. Inspection of the wreckage revealed that a crack in one of the propellers had caused the flyer to lose power on one side, creating stresses that twisted the vertical rudder out of position. Milton, however, cast the blame more widely. "I think your caution would have avoided the accident," he wrote Wilbur. Will, in turn, said as much in a letter to Katharine: "I can't help thinking over and over again, 'If I had been there, it would not have happened.'" Neither Milton nor Wilbur ever repeated this charge to Orville.

But the U.S. Army was blaming no one. Army officials did all they could for Orv and agreed to postpone flight tests until his full recovery. One officer was especially attentive. "Lieut. Lahm saved the day," Katharine wrote Will in mid-November, when she and Orv were finally back in Dayton. "I should have died if it hadn't been for him. He came out every night and was too decent for words."

The frequent mention of Lieutenant Lahm in Katharine's letters suggests that she was very fond of him, and he of her. They obviously admired each other tremendously. Perhaps the attraction ran deeper; at any rate, they became friends for life.

Lahm was one of the first to notice that Katharine was more than a sister to her brothers. At the end of his career, when he was a retired general, he reminisced about his first acquaintance with the Wright sister: "In my frequent visits to the hospital, I came to know and appreciate the sterling character of the third member of the team who was with them through the vicissitudes of those early days, sharing their hopes and disappointments."

Europe

K ATHARINE WAS PEEVED. "I wish you would come home," she begged Wilbur at the end of November 1908. "Nobody else takes a particle of responsibility. They leave everything on me. I am about played out but Orv doesn't realize it a bit. I think he wonders why I don't teach school."

Two weeks earlier Will had written suggesting that Orv, Katharine, and Milton come to Europe. Orv was well enough to have made the train trip home to Dayton at the end of October, so Will thought he might as well take the boat ride across the Atlantic, ideally with the rest of the family. He needed Orv's help with demonstration flights planned for the coming year in France and Italy, and he felt his father and sister would enjoy the sights. Furthermore, he wouldn't be home for Christmas and missed their company.

Katharine wasn't sure how seriously to take this invitation. She would love to go to Europe — she had never been farther east than Fort Myer — but she had also been without income since Orv's accident and was anxious to be self-supporting again. Orv thought it a simple matter for her to return to teaching. But according to the principal at Steele, Katharine's substitute was employed until the end of the semester, and Katharine would have to wait until after Christmas to return to work.

In early December, Will repeated his invitation and added a reason that would encourage his sister to accept: "We will be needing a social manager and can pay enough salary to make the proposition attractive, so do not worry about the six [dollars] per day the school board gives you for peripateting [strolling] about Old Steele's classic halls." A social manager would come in handy, since influential and famous people were now flocking to see the airplane, and Will and Orv didn't always have the patience to be nice to them. Above all, Katharine knew how to be nice.

Milton had just turned eighty and declined the invitation. He tried to influence Katharine to refuse also, but she couldn't bear *not* to go. She arranged for Carrie and her husband to take care of Milton, and she requested an extension of her leave of absence from Steele until the following September. This was a risky move, since the new superintendent might hire a permanent replacement at a lower salary. However, she was willing to take the chance.

On January 5, 1909, as the recuperating Orv hobbled up the gangway of a passenger liner in New York harbor, he was accompanied by his firm's new social manager. She was outfitted in a splendid traveling dress and hat. Packed in her trunks were two new evening gowns: one of pale dusty pink, the other of shimmering black. At age thirty-four, Katharine Wright was having a big adventure at last.

The voyage across took a week, but it took Katharine centuries back in time. She arrived in a world she later remembered as "like a dream." As hostess at 7 Hawthorn Street, she had entertained countless church friends of her father and held her own with everyone from aeronautical experts to Oberlin academics. These experiences hardly prepared her for meeting the illustrious European aristocrats and royals who came to see her brothers' invention,

Katharine and Orville with a helpful fellow passenger
during their ocean crossing in January 1909.

much less for being the person waited on rather than the waitress at these glamorous gatherings.

Aside from children, Katharine had never met people who had no occupation except amusing themselves. Apparently, the latest amusement in Europe was to come to Pau (pronounced "poe")—the resort city in southern France where Wilbur was conducting his latest flight demonstrations.

Orv and Katharine arrived in Pau on January 16, delayed by several hours because their passenger train collided with a freight train. Two people died in the crash and many were injured, but Orv and Katharine escaped unscathed. After the wreck, Katharine observed that French officials seemed helpless in the face of the emergency, unable to take action until they were given orders. This was completely contrary to the American practice, which was for everyone to rush in and take charge at once. Both approaches had their drawbacks, and Katharine was learning the lesson of all world travelers: that people and cultures differ in unexpected ways.

Not only would she survive a train wreck in France, she would later barely avoid injury in Italy when a too zealous car chauffeur steered her into a stone wall. But Katharine would have pleasant surprises too: among them, encountering Ohio friends at the Louvre Museum in Paris; discovering that Rome was "much more impressive" than even she expected; and being the recipient of countless flower bouquets, presented by chivalrous European gentlemen.

Wilbur had chosen Pau for its excellent flying field, its mild winters, and its persuasive town officials, who were eager to bring *l'homme-oiseau* to their community as a tourist attraction. They provided him with a combination hangar-private apartment, a personal chef, and a direct telephone line to town. Orv and Katharine were put up free of charge at the grand hotel next to the old royal castle where one of France's most popular kings, Henri IV, was born in 1553.

The hotel was even colder than Katharine's classroom at Steele, and her letters home almost shiver with protest about the stinginess with heat. The supposedly mild climate was "as cold as January," she wrote Milton in mid-February. "I never was so uncomfortably cold in all my life. . . . The 'oldest inhabitants' claim that it is very unusual but I have an idea that this sort of thing happens every year. Of course, the hotel is not prepared for the cold and as a consequence, we are freezing."

Orv spent most days with Will on the field, where flights commenced on February 3. Will or one of his students always served as pilot, since Orv was still too frail to risk being at the controls.

Wilbur aloft at Pau, France, 1909.

Katharine spent every morning at the hotel for a two-hour French lesson. Then she had lunch meetings — often conducted in French — with important social and business contacts for her brothers. Afterward she usually went to the flying field to meet other important people. Her job was to say *non*, as often as was polite, to requests for her brothers' attendance at teas, dinners, parties, and banquets. There were enough occasions when she had to say *oui* to make their social life interesting.

Milton disapproved of his children associating with frivolous high society, which he heard about from their unfailingly honest letters. Nonetheless, he saved his strongest condemnation for his sons' refusal to follow Katharine's example and master French. "What would you think of a Frenchman who would be in America almost a year and knows little of the language around him?" he chided Orv. "You would count him slow to learn, or too nice to live."

Wilbur (seated right) and pupil bank over horse-drawn carriages at the edge of the flying field at Pau, 1909. The pupil is French balloonist Paul Tissandier.

As social manager, Katharine was rubbing elbows with the sort of people she had previously encountered only in novels. There were counts and countesses, dukes and duchesses, lords and ladies. There was a marquis, a princess, and a former prime minister. At Pau, she even met two kings— Edward VII of England and Alfonso XIII of Spain. On the second leg of the trip they traveled to Rome, where she met King Victor Emmanuel III of Italy. By then she was getting blasé about the experience: "We have to bounce out early tomorrow morning and take the seven o'clock car to the country," she wrote Milton. "The King is to come at eight o'clock. The Kings are a nuisance all right. They always come at such unearthly hours."

Katharine's wide reading failed her when she tried to remember the protocol for addressing counts as opposed to, say, marquesses, or for making the thousand-and-one other distinctions of rank that were second nature to European courtiers. Before meeting King Alfonso, for example, she had to

Above, left: Orville, Wilbur, and King Edward VII of England, 1909.
Above, right: Katharine talks to King Alfonso XIII of Spain, as Orville looks on, 1909.

practice a proper curtsey under the guidance of the wife of an English baronet. However, when the time came, she couldn't help greeting the Spanish sovereign American style — with a friendly handshake and a pleasant smile. He was charmed.

American tourists were common in Europe, but it was unusual to encounter such unpretentious, dignified, and courteous people as the three visitors from Dayton. The press latched on to this endearing trio. Even so, the Wrights were dull by French journalistic standards, so reporters concocted a little mystery surrounding the family. Wilbur, for instance, was alleged to have stolen the wife of a lieutenant in the French army. When this fanciful tale got back to Dayton, friends quickly came to his defense, asserting that the charge couldn't possibly be true — as, of course, it wasn't.

The Gallic press was more gallant with Katharine. Her job as a high school Latin teacher sparked speculation that she was the calculating genius behind her brothers' invention. Latin and Greek were even more prestigious in France than in America, and the link between classical languages and mathematics was even stronger. It was obvious to all — at least in France — that only someone with the highest academic credentials could be responsible for such a technically difficult feat as the airplane, and in the Wright family that person was Katharine.

The grain of truth behind this flight of fancy was something that Lieutenant Lahm had realized: that the airplane was a family achievement and that Katharine was one of the indispensable members of the amazing Wright partnership.

Flying

FROM PAU the late afternoon sun was sinking toward the nearby Pyrenees Mountains. Wilbur had just finished a twenty-minute lesson with his student pilot Count Charles de Lambert. The calm, bright air on that February 15, 1909, beckoned him aloft again. He asked the count's wife if she would like to join him.

It was her fondest wish!

In four minutes' time they flew down the field and back.

Then as twilight approached, Wilbur asked his sister if she would care for a ride.

Of course!

Katharine slipped into the passenger seat next to the engine. As Will climbed in beside her, Orv tied her long coat with twine so it wouldn't flap in the breeze. She secured her hat. Then the engine roared to life, driving two noisy chains attached to propellers in the rear.

Draped in front of Katharine was a piece of string. This was the "deadman's" switch, designed so that a person lurching forward during a crash would press against the cord and stop the motor, which might otherwise start a fire.

Katharine ready for her first flight on February 15, 1909.
Women who flew at this time had their long skirts bound near the ankles,
which started the rumor that the stylish hobble skirt was inspired by the practice.
However, the designer responsible seems to have been influenced by Asian fashions.

Katharine steadied her feet against a small rail and grasped a wing strut with her hand. After making a final check, Will reached down and released a catch.

Quick as a wink, a weight dropped from a derrick and yanked the plane down its launch rail. Picking up speed, the vehicle stayed on the rail until Will eased back on a lever with his left hand, which caused the horizontal rudder to pivot . . . and suddenly they were airborne!

Or were they? The feeling was so subtle it was hard to tell. They were gliding upwards as if on a gravity-defying sled or on a track ascending into the sky. A brief dip, caused by the wind, told Katharine they were indeed supported by nothing but air itself. They were flying!

Will had a lever in each hand and made slight adjustments that guided them down the field at treetop height, going exactly where he wanted rather than where the wind or willful machine dictated.

It was an odd sensation. To Katharine the only clue that they were moving was the sight of the earth traveling backwards beneath them — that and the sting of cold air against her face. When they turned and reversed direction, the blast of air suddenly let up. It occurred to her that they were now traveling *with* the wind.

Will made a long circuit of the field. Then he cut the engine, and in eerie quiet they swooped toward the ground. Katharine felt light-headed as her brother guided the plane to the gentlest of landings. The flight had lasted all of seven minutes. "Them *is* fine!" she wrote Milton the next day, using a favorite Wright family expression.

A week later Wilbur took her up on a 13-mile flight over the surrounding countryside. "It was great," she reported to her father again, with an unmistakable passion for this new adventure.

King Alfonso XIII of Spain was not so lucky. When he came to Pau on February 20, he sat in the airplane for a long time talking to Wilbur. He wanted to know how everything worked, and he dearly wanted the machine to take off with him in it. But he had promised his queen and cabinet ministers that he would not ask for a ride.

When King Edward VII of England came on March 17, he was less curious than his Spanish colleague. He missed the first takeoff because he was chatting with a member of his entourage. To impress His Britannic Majesty, Wilbur took off again with Katharine as passenger, showing that even a gracious, well-dressed lady could fly unruffled through the air, as effortlessly as riding in a motorcar.

This time brother and sister stayed aloft for twelve minutes and twenty-two seconds. As Katharine grew more accustomed to the strange sensations of flight, her attention wandered from the deafening noise, the rush of air, the nervous jolts, and the tense concentration of the pilot. The scenery was breath-

Katharine, her hat tied, ready for a balloon ride with Orville (behind),
February 25, 1909.

taking! The field at Pau was on a broad plain that gradually ascended into the Pyrenees, whose snowy peaks brushed the purple sky about 20 miles distant. Katharine thought it was the most beautiful landscape she had ever seen.

In fact, she had enjoyed an even higher view a few weeks earlier, when she and Orv took a balloon ride from Pau to a mountain village 16 miles away. On being told in advance of this excursion, Milton had let his daughter know that under no circumstances should Wilbur go. "It does not make so much difference about you," he wrote, "but Wilbur ought to keep out of all balloon rides. Success seems to hang on him, in aeroplane business."

Katharine was used to her father's casual cruelty. Milton viewed the airplane as a business proposition, pure and simple, and he disapproved of anyone taking enjoyment from it or from any other sporting activity like

ballooning. "Make business first; pleasure afterward, and that guarded," he had chided her many years earlier.

As it happened, the bishop lacked even the self-restraint of the King of Spain. The following year, in May 1910, Orv managed to coax his father aboard a flight at Huffman Prairie. As Orv leveled off at a dizzying height of 350 feet his eighty-one-year-old passenger shouted, "Higher, Orville, higher!"

Reunion

I N MAY 1909 the Wright brothers and their social manager sailed home. From Pau they had gone on to Paris, then Rome, then Paris again, then London. There were flights in Pau and Rome only, and business meetings and banquets everywhere else. Not only were Wilbur and Orville now famous, they were rich, as one country after another signed up for deliveries of Wright airplanes.

In late June the U.S. Army resumed flight tests at Fort Myer. Before proceeding with these critical trials, the brothers had to dispense with a bout of public events. Dayton was making up for six years of neglect by throwing a two-day extravaganza of parades, dinners, speeches, and fireworks to honor its native sons. Even President William Howard Taft was invited, but he couldn't come. Not to be left out, he arranged a special reception at the White House. Held on June 10, this function was preceded by a lavish luncheon at Washington's exclusive Cosmos Club, which had to suspend its rule against women guests so that Katharine could attend.

While in town for these festivities, Katharine had a reunion with an old Oberlin friend. Harry Haskell was now Washington correspondent for the *Kansas City Star*. When he showed up at the hotel to interview Will and Orv, he was hoping to find her there as well.

High over Huffman Prairie, Bishop Wright takes his first airplane ride, May 25, 1910.

Katharine was delighted to see Harry. In excited fashion, she described how his name had come up the previous evening when she and her brothers were discussing a magazine article they had been reading on the train. The story repeated the French rumor that she was the secret mathematician behind the airplane.

"I told the boys that there was one person that would know it wasn't so!" she exclaimed. "The boys laughed, because they knew how I had depended on you to help me out in freshman math review."

Harry probably spent more time talking to Katharine than interviewing the brothers. He learned all about her recent life. And she learned about his. He was currently posted in Washington for the year, while Isabel was back in Kansas City with their seven-year-old son, Henry. The *Star* was notoriously stingy with salaries, but Harry was rising through the ranks of one of the most exciting news operations in the country.

At Oberlin he had been such a good math student that his friends were surprised when he went into journalism. But Harry's wide range of interests made it the perfect career for him. After graduating from college, he moved to Kansas City with an eye on a spot at the *Star*, which he landed only after toiling at a smaller paper for two years. At the time, Kansas City was just emerging from its frontier-era role as a jumping-off point for pioneers heading west. Its raw energy was transforming it into an important financial, political, and cultural center — with an ambitious newspaper to match.

The Wright-Haskell reunion also caught up on class news. Katharine's former fiancé, Arthur Cunningham, was now a surgeon in Washington State, married with two children. Her old roommate Harriet Silliman had finally found a teaching job; she rose to the post of principal and had recently married. Kate Leonard still lived in Oberlin, where she worked in the college library and took care of her father and invalid sister.

There was much else to discuss, but Katharine had to leave for the Cosmos Club, and from there for the White House. At Oberlin who would ever have thought she would have *that* excuse!

When she got to the Cosmos Club, Lieutenant Lahm was there. So was Alexander Graham Bell, inventor of the telephone and himself an aerial

*Flanked by notables, President William Howard Taft (center) poses with Wilbur
(on his right) and Orville and Katharine (on his left). The brothers hold gold medals,
bestowed for "keeping your nose right at the job until you had accomplished
what you had determined to do," said Taft.*

experimenter. The leaders of Congress came, along with many other important and powerful people.

Lunch adjourned at 2:15 P.M., and everyone walked the few blocks to
the White House. There, President Taft presented Wilbur and Orville with
gold medals on behalf of the Aero Club of America. Speeches were made, and
a formal portrait taken. The three Wrights flanked the president, along with
seven dignitaries. All were somberly attired except Katharine, who wore a
radiant white gown and a plumed hat. She stood next to Orv, and together
they looked a little like bride and groom, with the imposing president as minister. To the side, Wilbur could have been taken for best man.

Katharine ran into President Taft again a few weeks later, when he came
to Fort Myer to see the airplane. Ever the gentleman, he introduced himself in

case she didn't recognize him. "I met you at the White House," he reminded her. Katharine replied that she remembered him very well.

Trials

THE FORT MYER TRIALS proceeded without major mishap and concluded with a thrilling cross-country flight in which Orv left the safety of the parade ground and flew at top speed—about 40 miles an hour—to a hill 5 miles away. He then returned to the tumultuous honking of horns and wild cheers from spectators, aware that they had just witnessed the utility of this new technology. Airplanes could actually be used to go places—and not just circle a field endlessly. On August 2, 1909, the U.S. Army formally accepted its first airplane.

As far as Katharine was concerned, her fling with fame was now over. She was ready to retire from royal visits and presidential receptions and return to teaching. At Steele her colleagues had generously taught extra Latin classes to keep the superintendent from hiring a replacement. Come September, her job, classroom, and students would be waiting.

But once again the Wright firm needed her. Orv was sailing to Germany after the Fort Myer tests, but Will had business in the U.S. and couldn't go. So he asked Katharine to accompany Orv to handle the nobles, diplomats, and other celebrities expected—as usual—to flock to the flights. The trip meant missing at least a month of school, and Katharine knew that her job could not wait forever.

"I don't know what to do about the teaching," she wrote her old friend Agnes Osborn. "I don't want to drop out and yet I can't hold on to the place indefinitely." It was especially frustrating, since she had just returned from her first visit to Rome, ready to bring the ancient world more alive than ever to her students.

As so often in her life, she let others make the decision for her. No one could believe she wouldn't want to sail to Europe again; that she wouldn't gladly give up nine years in the classroom for a life as social manager to the most famous inventors in the world; that she wasn't thrilled by the fashionable people who courted her friendship abroad; that — in short — she wouldn't just drop everything and go. So she went.

In early July, a month before leaving, an unexpected encounter gave her something else to think about. She was at 7 Hawthorn Street managing the painting and wallpapering of the house during blistering summer weather. For several evenings the most distinguished temperance preacher in America, Dr. Howard Russell, dropped by to visit Bishop Wright. Dr. Russell was in town to organize against the evils of alcohol. During Katharine's college days he was already famous for having given up his career in law to attend Oberlin's religious seminary and start a campaign to shut down the nation's saloons. Many students signed his temperance pledge to forego liquor for life.

A spellbinding lecturer, Dr. Russell was strikingly handsome for his fifty-three years. He was also married with children. Therefore Katharine could not have been more shocked when he took advantage of their privacy after Milton went to bed to show his personal affection for her. "I had the weirdest experience," she confided to Agnes. "Would you ever imagine that I could let myself get wound up with a *married* man? Well, I did — and an Oberlin man, too, and a very well known man — old enough to be my father. Well, I wasn't altogether innocent, I fear, though I had sense enough to hold things down pretty well. It was like sitting on top of a volcano! The man isn't a bad man, in any way — only weak, because he has been away from home too much and was sick. I was so absolutely innocent about being friendly and he was fascinating — terribly bright and interesting. The first thing I knew he was altogether *too* interested in me. I should have kept him from coming out but I let things drift on until I finally came to my senses fully and sent him home — to the hotel. I won't be bad again. You'll forgive Katy, won't you?"

Dr. Russell got the message and apparently never bothered Katharine again, although for years afterward he showed up regularly at the Wright household. "Oh, we had the longest siege with Dr. Russell the other night. I don't care much for him," Katharine wrote a friend in 1925. "Dr. Russell was after money, of course," she added.

Will

BY EARLY 1912 the excitement of flight was finally wearing off at 7 Hawthorn Street. Will and Orv had succeeded beyond their wildest dreams, but now they faced a nightmare of litigation to protect their invention. Everyone, it seemed, was building airplanes based on the Wright model. The brothers didn't mind when flight enthusiasts tried out wing warping and other patented discoveries. But when experimenters turned into exploiters and started putting on shows for money or selling airplanes using Wright innovations — which no practical airplane could avoid — then lawyers for the Wright firm sprang into action.

The most persistent offender was the American aviator Glenn Curtiss, who tried everything he could think of to get around the Wright patents. In 1912 he argued that the brothers' mastery of steering was not original (it was) and therefore shouldn't be protected by a patent. Wilbur spent much effort fighting these and other attempts to deprive him and Orville of their hard-won discoveries and the right to profit from them.

"In the days of the invention it was all fun and no worry," the brothers would say, "but when we succeeded it was all worry and no fun."

By this time, Katharine had given up any hope of having a career. She had lost her place at Steele, and her brothers' business was on such a professional footing — with factories, workers, managers, secretaries, and a board of directors — that there was no longer an official role for her. So she spent much of her time doing volunteer work. She was a director of the Young Woman's League of Dayton, and she was active in feminist causes — notably in the national effort to win women the right to vote, a subject she raised so often that Orv teased it was "like Rome" to her, since all roads led to it in her conversation.

Katharine was not the only Wright committed to gaining women the vote. The bishop had long promoted the cause from the pulpit, and he and Orv both marched beside Katharine in a 1,300-strong parade through downtown Dayton in 1914. The preaching, demonstrating, and lobbying finally paid off in 1920, when the U.S. Constitution was amended with the sentence: "The right of citizens of the United States to vote shall not be denied or abridged by the United States or by any State on account of sex."

Milton may have been enlightened on this issue, but he often treated Katharine as if she were still a child. He was obsessed with her social life, and his diary documents an irrational suspicion of her appointments: "Mrs. Russell, Mrs. Guthrie, and Mrs. Stevens came in for gambling with Katharine," he noted about an innocent bridge game. "Katharine and Orville go to Miss Myer's to a party, against my protest. I hold late hours an infringement of the Sabbath," he complained about a Saturday night outing. "Agnes [Osborn] Beck, Winifred Ryder, and Miss Hunt 'dined' with Katharine and spent the evening. I ate almost nothing," he wrote about a meal that seems to have been a veritable Roman orgy in his imagination.

As fame and fortune settled on the Wright family their modest middle-class life at 7 Hawthorn Street was coming to an end: they were moving. Together, Will, Orv, and Katharine had picked out a 17-acre site in a nearby suburb where they planned to build a grand house in the style of southern mansions they had seen on their trips to Fort Myer. Katharine was to be mistress of this new home.

Will and Orv paid for the land in February 1912. Meanwhile, Dayton's most prominent architectural firm plunged ahead with plans for an estate that the Wrights would call Hawthorn Hill, after the many hawthorn trees on the property but also in tribute to their old home on Hawthorn Street.

In another sign of changing times, the Wrights were no longer front-page news, except for occasional headlines on the progress of their lawsuits. The big story in early 1912 was the admission of New Mexico and Arizona as the forty-seventh and forty-eighth states of the Union. Then in mid-April a new ocean liner called *Titanic* sank in the north Atlantic after hitting an iceberg. For the next few weeks newspapers wrote about little else, as the survivors arrived in port and their horrifying tales of the tragedy began emerging.

The press was still on the story in early May when Wilbur returned home from a trip to Boston. He was not feeling well and traced his indisposition to bad oysters eaten at his hotel.

That year there had been a number of outbreaks of typhoid fever in the Northeast linked to oysters collected in polluted waters. Local boards of health had the authority to seize contaminated food, close restaurants, and take other measures to control the disease. But the explosive growth of cities and the lack of proper sewage treatment made typhoid epidemics common. Boston's toll of typhoid victims had been declining steadily to a low of about 500 cases a year by 1912. Unfortunately, Wilbur was one of those cases.

In 1896 Milton had been out of town when Orville contracted typhoid, but he had told Katharine what to do by letter: "Put him in the best room for air and comfort. Sponge him off gently and quickly with the least exposure and follow with mild friction. . . . Boil the water you all drink, and set it in ice water to cool. Use the best economy about rest. Be temperate in articles eaten. Be regular."

Such care for the patient and precautions about preventing spread of the disease had worked for Orville, and it had worked again twelve years later when young Milton was stricken. But Wilbur's case was different.

On May 18, after more than a week of high fever, he slipped into unconsciousness. Knowing what might come, he had dictated his last will and testament. Milton documented the rest of the drama in his diary:

SATURDAY, MAY 18: *Wilbur is no better. He has an attack mentally for the worse. It was a bad spell. He is put under opiates. He is unconscious mostly.*

SUNDAY, MAY 19: *. . . He is mostly unconscious.*

MONDAY, MAY 20: *. . . Wilbur's case very serious. . . .*

TUESDAY, MAY 21: *. . . Wilbur seems a little better. . . .*

WEDNESDAY, MAY 22: *. . . The doctors think him better.*

THURSDAY, MAY 23: *. . . He seems about the same. This is the 21st day.*

FRIDAY, MAY 24: *Wilbur seems, in nearly every respect, better. . . .*

SATURDAY, MAY 25: *Wilbur seems a little better today.*

SUNDAY, MAY 26: *. . . Wilbur was worse in the night. . . .*

MONDAY, MAY 27: *Agnes Beck called. Reuchlin saw him in the*

afternoon. *I slept with my clothes on. We thought him near
death. He lived through till morning.*

TUESDAY, MAY 28: . . . *Wilbur is sinking. The doctors have no
hope of his recovery. . . .*

WEDNESDAY, MAY 29: *Wilbur seemed no worse, though he had a
chill. The fever was down, but rose high. . . .*

THURSDAY, MAY 30: *This morning at 3:15, Wilbur passed away,
aged 45 years, 1 month, and 14 days. A short life, full of
consequences. An unfailing intellect, imperturbable temper,
great self reliance and as great modesty, seeing the right clearly,
pursuing it steadily, he lived and died. Many called — many
telegrams. (Probably over a thousand.)*

Milton was deeply sad, but he had witnessed many deaths and preached
many funerals. His son's departure hurt him, but his summing up of Wilbur's
life shows that he perceived it as a complete and triumphant whole.

Katharine and Orv could not be so objective. Nothing since their
mother's death had prepared them for so great a loss. They were devastated
and took solace mainly from each other's company — though for weeks
Katharine walked around in a daze, not daring to start thinking or feeling. She
suspected Orv was in the same state.

The newspapers, too, saw the tragedy of Wilbur's passing. The co-
inventor of the airplane had died, not striving mightily in his machine, but
careworn and sick from a bad meal. The *New York Times* even found someone to blame: "Had not the members of some Board of Health neglected their
duties, Wilbur Wright would not have been attacked by typhoid; it is more
than possible that, if he had not been worn in mind and body by a ceaseless
legal battle to maintain the rights on which his livelihood depended, he could
have resisted and recovered from the fever. . . . There is something obviously,
even desperately, wrong in a state of affairs like this."

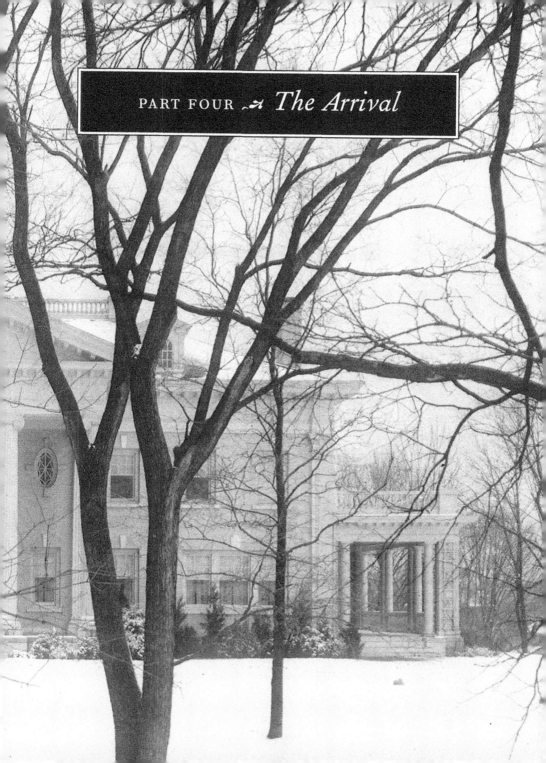

PART FOUR *The Arrival*

Orville, Katharine, and Milton (foreground) on the path at Hawthorn Hill, 1915.
Second from right is Horace, one of Lorin's children. The others are a family attorney and two journalists.

Previous pages:
Hawthorn Hill, where the Wrights moved in 1914, framed by winter branches.
Katharine's bedroom is on the second floor and includes the small balcony just above the main entrance.

Cal

O N OCTOBER 12, 1925, America's most reticent politician entertained the country's most reserved inventor. President Calvin Coolidge, "Silent Cal," was having Orville Wright over for lunch.

At age fifty-four, Orville was the grand old man of aeronautics. It had been twenty-two years since he and Wilbur first flew at Kitty Hawk, thirteen years since Wilbur died of typhoid fever, ten years since Orville sold the Wright Company for a rumored $1.5 million, and seven years since he last piloted an airplane.

He and Katharine resided at their mansion, Hawthorn Hill. Bishop Wright had lived with them for a few years after they moved in. Then one night in the spring of 1917 he died peacefully in his sleep. He was eighty-eight. Three years later Reuch, the oldest Wright brother, passed away at age fifty-nine — leaving Lorin, Orville, and Katharine as the surviving siblings.

Every few weeks Orv took trips to accept awards and attend meetings. Sometimes Katharine went with him, but mostly they stayed at home while the world came to them. Explorers, pilots, poets, professors, scientists, journalists, business tycoons, and politicians all came to Hawthorn Hill. Some, like Harry Haskell, were close friends and stayed a few days. Others just wanted to stop by and meet a living legend — the surviving member of the team that invented the airplane.

Lunch with President Coolidge was the finale of a weeklong trip that included air races in New York, banquets, receptions, and testimony before a special presidential board in Washington.

Katharine went along. In New York she shopped for china, attended a

Orville and Katharine (right) wave to crowds at the christening of the Wilbur Wright flying boat, 1922. Joining them are playwright Percy MacKaye (left), Arctic explorer Vilhjalmur Stefansson, and the pilot (seated).

play, and looked up friends. The night before Orv's testimony in Washington she helped him compose his remarks.

The board was interested in the future of aviation. The technology of flight had advanced so quickly that the president wanted advice on what he should do to encourage further development. Airplanes had played an important role in World War I, which had ended in 1918. In 1924 two U.S. Army planes had completed the first-ever flight around the world — a trip of more than fifty stops lasting just under six months. Airplanes were already carrying letters for the U.S. mail and passengers for newly formed airlines.

The board knew that Orville rarely spoke in public, but they wanted to be able to say they had consulted him. Orv obliged with a series of cautious recommendations. More airports were needed, he said. So were regulations

President Calvin Coolidge (in light suit) with his Aircraft Board, which solicited Orville's advice in October 1925. Third from left is board chairman Dwight Morrow, whose daughter Anne later married the celebrated aviator Charles Lindbergh.

to ensure the safety of airplanes and the proficiency of pilots. He avoided the subject of military aviation, since he had no idea what to expect. "The possibilities of the aeroplane for destruction by bomb and poison gas have been so increased since the last war, that the mind is staggered in attempting to picture the horrors of the next one," he had written two years earlier.

Orv talked for a few minutes and then answered questions. To Katharine's embarrassment, one of the board members drew attention to her. "We are hearing and have for years heard of the Wright brothers and their accomplishments," he announced, "but we hear very little of Miss Katharine Wright, who, after all, was just as instrumental in developing the airplane as were the brothers. I think we ought to at least be introduced to her. She is in the room."

Everyone looked at her and nodded respectfully.

It was a common myth that Katharine had done the math, sewn the fabric, paid the bills, or otherwise participated in some direct way in the development of the airplane. But her role had been more subtle. She said nothing to the board that day, but a few years earlier she had tried to scotch the rumors: "I did no pioneer work in connection with the invention of the aeroplane," she had written to an aviation magazine. "That pretty story was the outcome of someone's imagination. I had the greatest interest in my brothers' work always but that was all."

After the meeting, Orville and Katharine went to the White House. Katharine suspected that Harry Haskell had arranged the invitation through his Washington contacts. Harry was now chief editorial writer for the *Kansas City Star*.

Four other guests joined Orv and Katharine in the Coolidges' private dining room. One was the attorney general, John Garibaldi Sargent. Another was Lewis Strauss, a young banker and advisor to the secretary of commerce, Herbert Hoover (who would succeed Coolidge as president in 1929). Also attending were Mr. and Mrs. Jack Shaffer, an older couple from Chicago, where Mr. Shaffer owned a newspaper.

The Shaffers did most of the talking, and Katharine thought they acted annoyingly at home in the White House. Orville said nothing until the president asked him a few questions. Grace Coolidge, the president's wife, kept the ball of conversation rolling as best she could. Katharine thought her "intelligent, a good talker, and a hospitable hostess." Katharine found the president "sensible and quiet. . . . Of course he isn't exciting."

Katharine didn't record what was said, although she reported that the attorney general said very little and Mr. Strauss said nothing at all. She herself "made about three trite remarks."

Silent Cal's aversion to talk was renowned. He once told a friend: "Many times I say only 'yes' or 'no' to people. Even that is too much. It winds them up for twenty minutes more." According to one story, a young woman sitting next to him at dinner revealed that she had a bet she could make him say at least three words. "You lose," he replied.

After lunch the men retired to the library and the women to the drawing room. Eventually, the gathering broke up when the president announced he was going to a baseball game. The Washington Senators were playing the Pittsburgh Pirates in the fifth game of the World Series. A win for Washington would clinch the title. As it happened, they lost and Pittsburgh triumphed in the final two games.

Orville and Katharine left the White House feeling honored, but not exactly thrilled. They were exhausted from six days of nearly continuous activity. On an impulse they decided to leave that night instead of staying another day as planned. All they wanted now was to be back at Hawthorn Hill. Since they were too late to book lower berths on a sleeping car, they gladly settled for less convenient upper berths.

On the train home that evening other passengers might have mistaken the genial brother and sister for a contented, middle-aged married couple. They were so at ease in each other's company that nobody would have guessed that one of them was hiding something important from the other.

Harry

FOR THIRTY YEARS Katharine had considered Harry Haskell a dear friend, never realizing that he had secretly been something more at Oberlin. He had been in love with her.

At the time, he had concealed it so well that she didn't suspect a thing. To her he was a kind and generous upperclassman. "I always thought I was so lucky because you would be friends with me," she told him much later.

Then, as young hearts often do, he fell in love with someone else. This time romance blossomed. Harry and Isabel were married in 1901 after a five-year engagement. By then he was settled in a writing job at the *Star*, at a salary of fifteen dollars a week. A year later Henry was born.

The young family lived frugally in a rented cottage in Kansas City. Free theater tickets for reporters allowed them an occasional night out, with a neighbor volunteering to baby-sit. The Haskells owned the complete works of Charles

Harry Haskell with his sister, Mary, and their parents, before 1914.

Dickens, and over the years Harry read aloud all of the more than twenty volumes as his mesmerized wife and son munched popcorn to the escapades of Mr. Pickwick, the perils of Pip, and the heartrending ordeals of Little Nell.

Raised in a strict home that might have appeared in a Dickens novel, Harry loosened up under Isabel's influence. He learned to dance and play cards. He was already an enthusiastic singer, which he practiced every night while drying the dinner dishes.

As Harry advanced in his career the family was able to afford better housing and eventually a Model-T Ford. They moved into a new house they had planned for themselves. Shortly afterward, Isabel learned she had cancer. The disease spread slowly. After two years she was bedridden. Then on September 21, 1923, she looked up at her dear Harry and whispered, "It's been wonderful — all of it," and closed her eyes forever.

The death of his beloved wife plunged Harry into darkness and despair. Katharine wrote him often, trying to console him — unaware that her heartfelt letters might be rekindling an old infatuation.

Isabel and Henry, about 1903.

Harry in the late 1920s.

"I know all about the things you found so dark and forbidding when you got back to Kansas City," she wrote in March 1924 after he returned from a trip abroad to try to forget his loss. "Imagination is the hardest part to endure. When you can finally walk up to the dreaded thing it loses half its terror." She spoke from personal experience.

Katharine had the perfect touch. She could raise his spirits when he was down and tease him when he needed a laugh. She was merciless on the subject of Kansas City widows, who began planning parties for Harry with an eye toward matrimony. One was Arabella Hemingway, aunt of a promising young writer then living in Paris named Ernest Hemingway. In 1917 Harry had approved Ernest for a position at the *Star*, giving him his start as a professional writer.

Arabella and her competitors gave Harry a year and a half of mourning before trying to force his hand. In the spring of 1925, Katharine's letters took an alarmist turn when she got word from a Kansas City acquaintance that Harry might be ready to remarry. Assuming it was to one of the widows, she cautioned him, "Just watch your loneliness and make sure that you really want what you are drifting into." She was a little surprised at her directness on the subject. "I have wondered and wondered how I could help you get settled again," she explained later, "and I tried to hope you would find some real companionship — though I was worried when it came over me that maybe I was wanting you to keep free from entangling alliances, at least partly because I foresaw an end to the kind of a relation we have been growing into these last two years. I didn't want to be guilty of such selfishness as that."

Their correspondence grew more frequent, and soon they were writing every four days — the round-trip time for a letter and its reply between Dayton and Kansas City. Luckily, they had a subject that let them write often without acknowledging any deepening feelings: Harry was working to expose a plot against Wilbur and Orville's reputation as inventors of the airplane.

Charles Walcott, who had become head of the Smithsonian Institution after Langley's death in 1906, could not bring himself to admit that the Wright brothers had succeeded where his predecessor had failed. In 1914 he allowed Glenn Curtiss to modify Langley's flyer so it could actually fly — something it had never done. Curtiss's motive, as always, was to undermine the brothers' patent claims by arguing that their work was not original.

With major modifications, Langley's machine *did* get off the ground, though this feat did nothing for Curtiss's legal case, which he eventually lost. Nonetheless, the public began to get the idea that the Wright brothers might not have been the true pioneers of the airplane.

In 1925, Walcott capitalized on this misunderstanding by displaying Langley's flyer at the Smithsonian Museum with a label claiming it was the world's first airplane "capable" of flight. The label sounded impressive until one thought about the wording. How many thousands of sea captains and vessels were *capable* of sailing to America before Columbus? How many countless doctors were *capable* of discovering a smallpox vaccine before Jenner? If "capable" was the new standard — ignoring the fact that Langley's unmodified flyer wasn't capable of anything — no achievement in history was safe from the assertion that someone or something else was capable of it beforehand.

Through his editorials in the *Star*, Harry helped combat this injustice.

Raymond H. Stetson, head of Oberlin's psychology department and a close friend of Harry's, 1920s.

Exploring confusing matters in print came second nature to him; exploring the confused state of his own heart did not. As his love for Katharine rekindled, he asked an old friend at Oberlin for advice on what to do. Raymond H. Stetson, head of Oberlin's psychology department, had known Harry since their college days; and he had gotten to know Katharine through her activities for the college, especially since her election to the Oberlin board of trustees in 1923. As a psychologist and lifelong bachelor, Stetson felt he was a dispassionate observer of human relations.

"I believe it's ordinarily supposed to be a compliment to [a] woman to tell her that you like her that way; she'll be glad to know that it's still possible," he wrote Harry on June 8 in his idiosyncratic shorthand, which had various vowels and consonants removed (here restored).

The next day he continued his analysis: "I've no notion what she means to do—how things stand—but it's evident that she has some interest, that it's not a closed matter or she wouldn't rouse all this for herself and you. 'Course, I know how wild the most sane folk can be in this kind of thing. . . . "

Katharine (center), as an Oberlin trustee, at the 1924 graduation.

In other words, Stetson thought Katharine knew very well where their relationship was leading and had done nothing to stop it.

The psychologist continued, "And I must say that if I were you, I shouldn't wait till some summer camping trip [to propose marriage]. You can't afford emotional sprees of this sort, and why wait!"

An added consideration for Harry was how Orville would react. "Do you suppose," Stetson ventured, "if he were to be attacked by general emotionality and want to bring a wife into his life, that he'd hesitate? . . . I've no idea if Miss W. would take the risk and marry you; that's up to her; but I don't see anything in her present position that would make it impossible. 'Orv' isn't an aged parent or an invalid and semi-insane sister. . . . "

Emboldened by this advice, Harry made his move.

Katharine

KATHARINE WAS ONLY THE SECOND WOMAN ever elected to Oberlin's board of trustees. She took her duties very seriously — unlike many of the male trustees, who showed up unprepared and voted for whatever policy the president of the college recommended.

One of Katharine's causes was that women faculty members should be paid the same as men. Another was to recognize prominent women in the awarding of honorary degrees. Yet another was to stop the college from spending beyond its means and expecting trustees to make up the deficit out of their own pockets. Some trustees could afford this practice, but not Katharine. Will had left her $50,000 after his death, which was enough to make her independent but not enough to pay the college's bills.

These and other issues were on her mind when she arrived in Oberlin on Thursday, June 11, 1925, for the long graduation weekend. She would attend a daylong meeting of the trustees, plus assorted commencement festivities. She would also catch up with old friends — which she was in the process of doing on Friday when a telegram came to her hotel room while she was chatting with Kate Leonard.

As Kate looked on, Katharine read silently:

KANSAS CITY, MO. JUNE 12
MAILED IMPORTANT LETTER YESTERDAY AND TWO BY SPECIAL
DELIVERY TODAY WHICH SHOULD REACH YOU SATURDAY.
BUT IT IS SO MUCH MORE SATISFACTORY TO TALK THINGS
OVER I WONDERED WHETHER WE MIGHT NOT SPEND SUNDAY
IN CHICAGO MEETING AT THE BLACKSTONE HOTEL IN THE
MORNING. PERHAPS YOU WILL WANT TO SEE LETTER
TOMORROW MORNING BEFORE REPLYING.   H. J. HASKELL

Katharine scanned the message with growing confusion and alarm. What could it mean? She spent the rest of her visit with Kate trying to pretend that nothing of note was happening. That night she got very little sleep.

The next morning Harry's important letter was waiting at the hotel desk. But before she could read it, she had to meet Professor Stetson in the lobby. And before that meeting got under way, Harry's sister, Mary — who lived in Oberlin — dropped by. Katharine stuffed the letter into her handbag so that neither of them could see the handwriting.

After Mary departed, Katharine and Stetson talked about Orv's troubles with the Smithsonian. Stetson believed that Orv should write a complete account of his and Will's discovery of the airplane, something neither brother had ever done. Katharine agreed and wished that Will were still alive, since he would have taken care of it as soon as Walcott began muddying the waters of history. The fact that very little of the brothers' work was published left them vulnerable to such fraudulent claims.

When this topic was exhausted, Katharine asked Stetson if he didn't think it strange that Harry had not yet settled down with one of the Kansas City widows. Stetson replied that he didn't think it strange at all. Feeling self-conscious, Katharine let the subject drop.

When she was finally alone, she took a deep breath, slit open the letter, and started to read.

Confusion

STETSON WAS WRONG ABOUT KATHARINE. She had *no* idea where her intimate correspondence with Harry was leading. And when she read of his love for her that stretched back to their Oberlin days, she was stunned. "I didn't understand at all at first what you were hinting at," she wrote him that evening. "I guess you've got it through my head at last and I'm as nearly 'stricken dumb' as I'll ever be."

In his letter, Harry proposed marriage in the kindest, gentlest, most persuasive and romantic way, calling it a "great adventure" that awaited them. But it was an adventure that Katharine had put out of her mind years earlier, and she had never even dreamed of taking it with Harry.

She immediately wired him that a meeting in Chicago was not a good idea. She didn't want Orv to know about it, and she feared he would somehow find out. Later that night, at 11:15, she poured out her heart. "When I have sense enough to think *anything*," she wrote her surprise suitor, "I wonder who it is walking around here in Oberlin. I'll never forget *this* Commencement, that's sure."

Katharine was so unselfish that it was easy to miss her one area of inflexibility: her family. For her, Orville always came first, and she felt her mind swim as she tried to explain this.

"But, Harry," she continued, "you break my heart. I feel as if everything I had tried to be and do was tumbling down around me. I can't understand what has happened. And I feel to blame because I can't change my feeling, but it would be even worse if I could. I am sure no one can imagine how inseparable the relation is now between Orv and me. It would have almost killed me if he had, in these latter years, wanted someone else more than me. I can't desert him now, even if I could adjust myself to a change of feeling between us. I have taken care of him so much — I have lived in his life so long — I have felt so responsible about steering things here and there to smooth this way and that for him — I *love* him so, Harry — and we are so happy together. Since Will and Father have been gone we have been everything to each other. And he is so good to me. You would be good — I know that. I wouldn't be afraid for myself. That isn't it. But I haven't changed my feeling about you. It is all a dream to me that you have such feelings about me. I can't realize it."

She kept writing until almost one o'clock in the morning. Later she would call this her "crazy letter."

Katharine and Harry were now sending telegrams, special delivery letters, and regular letters several times a day — far faster than they could get replies.

She was horrified at the dilemma she faced. "Harry, how can I tell where affections leave off and love begins?" she wrote the day after her crazy letter. " . . . I don't *know* you, as you are now. I don't see that I could ever leave Orv but let me talk to you. It just *breaks my heart* to have you send such a telegram. 'It's all right. Please don't worry' etc. Of course it *isn't* all right and, of course,

I *will* worry. So I have sent you an answer and asked you to come — but I don't know myself to *what* I have asked you to come. Don't come if you will be more upset that way. Please Harry, don't care so much — and please *do!*"

The plan was for Harry to come to Dayton on Wednesday, June 17, a day after Orv left for an appointment in Philadelphia. Katharine would tell Orv that Harry was stopping by on a trip east — as he often did. They would then be free to talk in private without seeming surreptitious. However, this rendezvous fell through when Orv got 15 miles outside of Dayton only to realize he had left his ticket, money, identification, and all his work papers at home. He decided to call off the trip. When Katharine found out, she was panic-stricken and quickly phoned the telegraph office to relay the news to Harry, who called off *his* trip.

"I believe you have to begin younger than we are to arrange for these secret (!) meetings," she wrote Harry that night. "This one certainly was torpedoed in the most unaccountable way."

Fortunately, Orv had a meeting in Washington the following week. Katharine let her brother know that Harry's rescheduled trip just happened to coincide with his, except they would overlap for a few hours on Orv's return. This plan went off as scheduled. Orv left on Wednesday, June 24, came back on Friday, found Harry at Hawthorn Hill, had a short visit, and then didn't notice a thing when Harry and Katharine exchanged meaningful glances at their parting.

"I am afraid if Orv's eyes had been sharp, he would have seen in that expression on your face when you said goodbye to me, something different from anything he'd seen before," she wrote the next day.

During this visit Katharine sensed something change. Before, she wasn't sure if her admiration and affection for Harry was love. She had never forgotten the day at Oberlin when he walked her home from chapel to tell her how glad he was that she had won the history prize for her essay on the Monroe Doctrine. Here he was, the smartest member of the senior class and the winner of many such prizes, yet he wanted her — a sophomore — to know that he was impressed and happy for her. This sincere gesture was the best prize of all. After Harry and Isabel married, Katharine had cut back on her letters to Harry, since she didn't think it was proper for a woman to correspond with a married man; not that she had any illusions, for ever since her failed engagement to Arthur Cunningham she had believed that men just weren't interested in her, except as a friend. When Isabel lay dying, Katharine did what a true friend would and came to Kansas City to comfort them both. Later, Isabel's death meant that Harry needed her friendship more than ever. But now he was asking something beyond friendship. Katharine decided that the only way to tell if she could give it was to test her feelings when they met again in person. She *wanted* to love him, as he apparently loved her. But she wouldn't know for sure until she felt her heart tell her something—*what*, she wasn't sure—that was definite, eternal, and different.

It did.

The Kiss

K ATHARINE AND HARRY had their first kiss on an island in Lake Huron while Orv was out fishing. She later recalled of Harry's stay, "It was a blessed, perfect two weeks."

Orville bought Lambert Island in 1916 after falling in love with the rugged scenery of Canada's Georgian Bay, a vast arm of Lake Huron bordering Ontario. Starting in 1918, he and Katharine spent two months every summer at the island, which comprised 26 acres, three simple cottages, a toolhouse, icehouse, pump house, and boathouse.

Harry arrived during the last week of July 1925. Orv and Katharine met him at the train station on the mainland, and then transported him 12 miles to the island in Orv's boat powered by an old airplane engine. Orv thought his guest looked "jumpy" and in need of a rest.

Harry was assigned the guest cottage, nestled in a rocky nook about 300 feet from the main house, which was sited atop a 100-foot-high hill. The main house had a kitchen, living room, screened porch, and a small bedroom where Katharine stayed. It also had cooling breezes and a magnificent view of water

Katharine on Lambert Island, about 1920.

and islands in all directions, best experienced from a big easy chair. Orv had his own small cottage nearby.

Lambert Island was Kitty Hawk reborn to Orville. Unlike the vacation homes of other millionaires, Lambert Island had no electricity, no bathrooms, no servants, no yacht, no dress code, and no pressure to conduct business. Rustic camp life reigned — though perhaps not as rustic as at Kitty Hawk.

While Orv was occupied with island improvements, Katharine kept house, prepared meals, swam, read, and wrote letters. Once a week she and Orv took the boat to town to get provisions, pick up mail, and fetch the occasional guest, such as Harry. Visitors were appreciated, as long as they were self-reliant and good conversationalists.

In this respect, Harry was perfect. Orv told Katharine that he thought him an able and conscientious man "with not a bit of conceit." Orv welcomed him almost like a member of the family, little suspecting that one day soon he might be just that.

It was strangely difficult for Katharine and Harry to steal time alone on their desert island. Orv usually suspended his projects when he had company. For someone so closemouthed in public, he was amazingly chatty and entertaining in private. He was an enthusiastic host, who liked to take his guests on long boat rides to find picnic spots and witness the beautiful sunsets on the bay.

Katharine's strategy was to suggest activities that didn't particularly appeal to Orv. Blueberry-picking was one — made all the more ideal because it could expand to fill almost any amount of time. Alone with Harry on these expeditions, during which they returned with surprisingly few berries, Katharine had so much to say to her lover that she often ended up saying nothing at all. Harry was similarly shy and was inclined to communicate his feelings poetically. He told her that he felt "home at last," alluding to the epitaph of one of their favorite writers, Robert Louis Stevenson:

Home is the sailor, home from the sea,
And the hunter home from the hill.

As with so much else in their relationship, Stevenson was a link to their Oberlin days, when Harry had sent her a book by the Scottish author as a graduation present.

But their most perfect communication didn't involve words at all. It took place in the big chair at the main house on afternoons when Orv was down at the dock fishing. Orv probably assumed that Harry didn't care for the sport. But up at the house his guest and sister were blissfully entwined in each other's arms, oblivious to the magnificent view of water and islands all around. "I *loved* your sitting there on that porch, not seeing how to 'get started,'" she teased him afterward. "It was natural enough for me to be tender with you....I *did* know what to do for once."

By the end of his stay on August 11, Harry and Katharine were of one mind: they had agreed to get married, and Katharine would find a way to tell Orv as soon as possible.

Orv

ORV'S CUSTOM whenever he walked in the door at Hawthorn Hill was to search the house until he found Katharine: living room, trophy room, library, kitchen, breakfast room, dining room, north veranda, south veranda—wherever he tracked her down, he was always happy to see her. Starting in the summer of 1925, he found her more and more often in her bedroom, writing letters.

He thought nothing of it. Neither did he think much about her frequent trips to the post office, her intense interest in mail deliveries, or her nearly constant state of agitation. One evening after dinner she sat looking through an album of photographs. Orv didn't realize that the pictures were of Harry's house in Kansas City and that she was studying her new home.

Katharine kept waiting for the perfect moment to tell Orv, but it never seemed to come. Two months after Harry's visit to Lambert Island, she and Orv made their long train trip to New York and Washington, during which they met President Coolidge. Cut free from the routine of Hawthorn Hill, she might have seized the moment to break the news. But she didn't.

Two months later, on December 17, she wrote Harry about his forth-coming visit for the holidays. She had told Orv that Harry *might* stop by for a few days after a Christmas Eve reunion in Oberlin with his sister, Mary. Orv was delighted. It never crossed his mind that the visit could be connected to the old tradition of announcing family weddings at Christmastime.

But now Katharine was having second thoughts. "I'd rather tell him after you are gone, dear," she wrote Harry. "I don't imagine it has ever occurred to him that I would or could leave him now. . . . "

After Christmas she kept delaying. "I suppose what will finally drive me to tell Orv will be a strain I can't stand any longer," she wrote on January 12. "How can I ever tell him feeling as I do? You see, dear, I know the look that will come over his face. He has always depended upon me when he is hurt or troubled—or, at least I have always been something of a comfort to him. . . . Maybe Orv doesn't want me as much as I think he does!"

In a letter to Harry, Professor Stetson had also considered the issue of Katharine and Orv's mutual dependence. "Of course," he explained, "she's been much to 'Orv' and probably is apt to exaggerate her indispensability; we do." Stetson further believed that Orv had more than reciprocated for his sister's devotion and had given her "a chance to be something and somebody."

Still, there was no reason Orv should prevent her from following her heart's desire. "If I were he," the professor mused, "I should say, 'go and be happy, if the thing's on you. You have me blessing; and in any case I don't want to be the occasion of one of these fine martyring devotions; not for me; goodbye and God bless ye.'"

Winter gave way to spring, and still Katharine delayed. By April friends in Oberlin and Kansas City were beginning to guess the truth about the romance. Harry had scheduled a trip east in May — a *real* business trip this time — and he planned to stop in Dayton.

"You'll have to talk to Orv when you are here — all by yourself, too," Katharine told him. "I'll cry if I am around and I don't want to do that, dear."

On May 13, 1926, Harry finally broke the news. Orv was so quiet that Harry wasn't sure how he was taking it. But when Katharine joined them, she saw the look on her brother's face and knew immediately that her worst fears were realized.

Katharine sometimes described Orv as being like a little boy: "It is his hurt look I can't stand — his appealing look — the look he always gives me when anything hurts him." Now, with the news that she wanted to marry, he had that look. After Harry left the next day, Orv descended into a deep depression, dragging Katharine down with him.

"I have done an awful thing," she wrote Harry in despair.

"I love you . . . whatever happens," he replied.

Over the next few weeks nothing much did happen, and Orv began to cheer up, believing that his show of suffering had convinced Katharine to give up her plan. But the wheels had been set turning. Katharine felt the familiar tug of family ties in one direction and her heart's eager yearning in the other. Orv assumed that she would put the family first, as she always had. Harry asked only that she listen to her heart.

He sent her a long telegram recalling his delayed trip to Dayton the previous summer: "I told you I wanted to help you find out what was in your heart. I haven't changed since and I couldn't possibly ask you to do what you thought you shouldn't. . . . "

Katharine was more agitated than ever, certain that the rest of the family would condemn her for abandoning Orv. But when Lorin and his wife, Netta, found out, along with Reuch's widow, Lou, they were thrilled. Netta and Lou immediately took Katharine in hand to help arrange the wedding.

Katharine hadn't picked a date or made any plans. Hawthorn Hill had been the scene of several family weddings, and she imagined hers taking place there as well. She wanted to keep it simple, though she could easily think of forty people to invite. She asked Lou to play the piano and Netta's daughter Ivonette to sing. The event was tentatively set for late November. All that was needed was the cooperation of the host — Orv.

Lorin volunteered to reconcile his brother to what was really a happy occasion for the entire family. But Orv was as stubborn as the newspaper editor Lorin had approached twenty-three years earlier with news of the first flight. Like that editor, Orv just could not be convinced. He didn't want Katharine to marry; he didn't want it to take place at his house; he didn't want his name connected with it in any way; and if she went ahead, he didn't want anything to do with her ever again.

Together

THE DAYTON JOURNAL *Saturday, November 20, 1926*

MISS KATHERINE WRIGHT IS TO WED HENRY J. HASKELL, KANSAS CITY STAR EDITOR

License for the marriage of Henry J. Haskell, chief editorial writer of the Kansas City Star . . . and Miss Katherine Wright . . . sister of Orville and Wilbur Wright, inventors of the airplane, was issued in Montgomery County probate court Wednesday. . . .

The marriage ceremony, which probably will take place today, will be conducted by Dr. H. C. King, president of Oberlin College....

The plans of the couple have been shrouded in the deepest secrecy. ... Mr. Haskell came to Dayton several days ago and went to Oberlin where the ceremony was expected to take place yesterday.

Dr. King, however, last night asserted that the marriage had not been performed, but declined to state when it would occur. Mr. Haskell, when questioned last night, asserted: "I am not married, but I will not say that I will not be within the next 24 hours." He refused to comment further.

Lorin and Orville Wright, brothers of Miss Wright, could not be reached last night and it was believed by friends that they had left the city, possibly to attend the marriage of their sister....

Those who have been acquainted with the friendship of Mr. Haskell and Miss Wright were not surprised to learn their long friendship had ripened into a matrimonial venture....

Miss Wright is internationally known as one of the three members of the Wright family who made the invention of the airplane possible.

ON NOVEMBER 20, 1926, at four o'clock in the afternoon, Katharine and Harry were married in the Oberlin home of their friends Louis and Frannie Lord, whom they had known since their college days. Only a few family members and friends attended. Orv was not among them.

Katharine never saw Hawthorn Hill again. Carrie took care of Orv, and she wrote Katharine often to let her know how he was faring. Katharine stayed in touch with a few other friends in Dayton, notably Agnes Beck, formerly Agnes Osborn.

Ten weeks after the wedding, Katharine wrote Agnes about her new life in Kansas City: "I hadn't supposed any one could be so good to me as Harry has been. He is so concerned over having brought me away from all my family and friends. It is very pleasant here, in every way. The house is pretty and comfortable and we have pretty much made it over inside."

The house had been a disaster before she arrived—the sort of place only a bachelor could occupy. Katharine was slowly putting it to rights with new wallpaper, new furnishings, new linens, and new dishes. In the meantime, the newlyweds were accepting invitations out. Katharine enjoyed Harry's friends, who were an interesting mix of writers, artists, politicians, and eccentric professionals—such as a doctor–big-game hunter.

But she still felt uprooted. "Your letter made me homesick," she confessed to Agnes on March 11, 1927. "In my imagination I walk through that house, looking for Little Brother, and at all the dear familiar things that made my home. But I never find Little Brother and I have lost my old home forever, I fear."

She was irritated with Orv more than angry. Apparently, in his mind she no longer existed. He had expelled her from the family as thoroughly as he had banished Langley from the honor roll of aviation pioneers. Sometimes she couldn't help feeling he was justified in his treatment of her. "Please write again when you can. I haven't had many letters. I suppose pretty much everybody was offended," she entreated Agnes.

Orv's life of leisure, honors, and chronic warfare with the Smithsonian continued. He rebuilt the airplane that first flew at Kitty Hawk and sent it to the London Science Museum to spite the Smithsonian for its refusal to change the label on Langley's machine.

In June 1927, Orv hosted the newly famous pilot Charles Lindbergh at Hawthorn Hill. The previous month Lindbergh had thrilled the world by flying solo from New York to Paris. For all his pluck, Lindbergh was no more daring than Orville or Wilbur had been. Yet he became the national hero they never were.

Meanwhile in Kansas City, Harry and Katharine were flying high in a different way. That summer brought a momentous change at the *Star*. The chief owner had died and his stock was sold to employees, achieving Harry's dream of a newspaper controlled entirely by the people who put it out. In fact, Harry became one of the paper's principal owners and one of its top three executives. "Really, Agnes," marveled Katharine, "it is another fairy tale—something like what our family went through once before."

Harry's son, Henry, was also in the newspaper business, as a reporter for the *Baltimore Sun*. Many grown-up children who see a parent remarry resent the new spouse. Not Henry. He considered Katharine "an angel" and thought her marriage to his father one of the happiest unions he could imagine. Above all, he was certain that Isabel would have approved.

Henry was another of Katharine's correspondents, and she kept him up to date on the transformation she was making in his boyhood home. They also discussed family finances, on which she had this advice: "My brother Will used to say that the difference between being rich and poor was the difference between having a little ahead and being a little behind." At the moment she was a little behind, since she was paying off a $5,000 pledge made to Oberlin to establish a scholarship in memory of her beloved Margaret.

Katharine's last letter to Agnes was on February 21, 1929. She had recently returned from Minnesota with Harry, where he had undergone surgery. He was recovering nicely—although any operation was dangerous, as Katharine reminded Agnes by reporting the recent death of a mutual friend who had contracted an infection after a routine appendectomy. Katharine herself had caught a cold and was finding it difficult to shake. "It is sad to get old," she wrote, in reference partly to herself, partly to their ever-shrinking circle of friends.

But warmer climes beckoned. On March 9, Katharine and Harry were due to board a ship for Italy and Greece—the classical lands that had inspired her studies at Oberlin and her years of teaching at Steele. Katharine had been to Italy once before: in 1909 with Will and Orv, when King Victor Emmanuel III came out in the early morning to see Will fly in a lovely field near Rome. From Italy, she and Harry would sail to Athens where they would meet up with the Lords—the couple who had volunteered their home for the impromptu wedding that had joined Katharine's past and future, linking the happy realm of her youth with an exciting, unknown adventure to come.

It was not to be. The bad cold turned into pneumonia. At the end of February, for the second time in his life, Harry began the death vigil for his dear spouse. He and Katharine had been married just two years and three months. She was fifty-four.

Soon Lorin was on his way from Dayton. Harry asked Katharine if she also wanted to see Orville.

"He may come if he wishes," she replied.

He arrived on Saturday, March 2, a day before the end.

Harry brought him into her room. "Here is Orv, Katharine. Do you recognize him?"

"Yes, of course," she whispered.

Orville never spoke of his own reaction. Perhaps he remembered another time when she lay helpless before him. It was on August 19, 1874, his third birthday. He was taken upstairs at Hawthorn Street to meet his new baby sister. He loved to tell Katharine that story, and he always added, "I saw then I was getting into trouble, and I've never got out since."

Brother and sister, 1915.

Epilogue: The Fountain

THREE U.S. ARMY PLANES dropped roses on Katharine's grave as she was laid to rest in Dayton's Woodland Cemetery on a sunny Wednesday afternoon. In life she had often visited the spot, since Susan, Milton, and Wilbur were buried there.

Orville and Harry had followed the hearse out from Hawthorn Hill, trailed by a procession of grieving family members and friends. At the service they had heard the pastor quote St. Paul: "Neither death, nor life, nor angels, nor principalities, nor powers, nor things present, nor things to come, nor height, nor depth, nor any other creature" could hold back heavenly love. No mention was made of Katharine's life or her unique spirit, which is probably the way she would have wanted it.

That task was left for Kate Leonard. A few months later her tribute to Katharine appeared in the *Oberlin Alumni Magazine*.

"When her classmates think of Katharine Wright," she wrote, " . . . they recall her unfailing good cheer, her love of good fun and her merry laughter. More and more, her fine friendliness, the largeness and loveliness of her life and service have been a source of pride and inspiration to them."

Kate was an astute observer of Katharine's role in the airplane: "[A]fter her brothers made their first successful flight in 1903 her intense and intelligent interest in their work and their desire for ventures into the outside world led her to give up her school work. In all their earlier experiments the boys had her confidence and encouragement and she now served them with an increasing and absorbing devotion. . . . Through all their varied experiences, Katharine had a great time as her brothers' 'social secretary' — but how much more than that she was, with all her gracious womanliness!"

Later in the long remembrance Kate wrote: "In November, 1926, Katharine Wright was married to Mr. Henry J. Haskell. . . . During these two years she had made many friends in her new home, her counsel was sought in personal and professional problems and, as in her Dayton home, her interest was aroused and her strength expended in many forms of public service."

She closed: "With all her strength and sincerity, born of strong convictions and lofty purposes, there was always a keen and tender sensitiveness to the needs and pain of others and, as a friend, it was her gentleness that made her great."

Kate herself did not have long to live. She died of heart failure during an operation just two years later. One of her classmates noted that she had "suffered terribly when Katharine died."

Life moved on. Orville flourished in retirement for another nineteen years. Only after his death in 1948 did the 1903 flyer return to America from London for display at the Smithsonian Museum.

Harry's remaining years were more eventful. A year after Katharine died, he was elected to Oberlin's board of trustees. In 1933 and again in 1944 he won journalism's highest award, the Pulitzer Prize, for his editorials educating readers to the crisis in Europe and America's responsibility to be a world leader. Along the way he found time to write two books about the relevance of the ancient world to the modern: *The New Deal in Old Rome* and *This Was Cicero*.

He also fell in love again and remarried. This time it was to Agnes Lee Hadley, the gentle, music-loving widow of a former Kansas governor. They had fifteen years before death took Agnes in 1946. Harry died six years later, in 1952.

Shortly after his third wedding, Harry presented Oberlin with a gift in memory of Katharine. It was a replica of a Renaissance monument they might have seen if they had made their European trip. In the mid-1400s the Italian artist Andrea Verrocchio, teacher of Leonardo da Vinci, had created a delightful bronze statue of a winged boy playfully clutching a dolphin. Later it was installed atop a marble fountain in the courtyard of the imposing Palazzo Vecchio in Florence. Now an exact copy of the fountain was to grace the front of Oberlin's art building, bearing the inscription:

TO KATHARINE WRIGHT HASKELL 1874–1929

In Verrocchio's day connoisseurs marveled at the realism of the boy. He seemed alive with energy, as if he were actually in mid-flight. As with many

Katharine Wright Haskell Memorial Fountain, Oberlin College.

Renaissance masterpieces, it was difficult to say what it meant. Was the boy Eros, the god of love, or was he an innocent cherub? Was he stealing the dolphin, or protecting it? Was the animal an augury of good luck, or a symbol of salvation?

And then there were the wings—so feathery and supple, defying the brittle material from which they were made. They were a mystery too. Wilbur and Orville might have said they were all wrong and that the boy could never fly.

But he did.

Author's Note

IN 1990 ONE OF MY JOBS was writing the exhibit labels for the Virginia Air and Space Center, then nearing completion in Hampton, Virginia. Among the airplanes, rockets, space vehicles, and other impressive artifacts was a dingy piece of cotton cloth, about 2 inches square. It was certainly historic: it had been part of the original wing covering of the 1903 Wright flyer. But I felt I had to say something extra to bring it alive next to its imposing competitors.

I did a bit of research in Fred Howard's biography of the Wright brothers, *Wilbur and Orville,* and came across the perfect passage. It was from a letter describing the brothers working with identical material on one of their earlier machines:

> *The flying machine is in process of making now. Will spins the sewing machine around by the hour while Orv squats around marking the places to sew. There is no place in the house to live but I'll be lonesome enough by this time next week and wish that I could have some of their racket around.*

The author was Katharine Wright; someone I didn't know existed. I used this haunting description in the label, and made a mental note to look up more letters by this eloquent member of the Wright family when I had a chance. What was her story?

Years went by. One day I thought about Katharine again while consulting the standard editions of Wright letters and papers: *Miracle at Kitty Hawk,* edited by Fred C. Kelly, and *The Papers of Wilbur and Orville Wright,* edited by Marvin W. McFarland.

What did these books have in the way of her correspondence? Not much, it turned out: among their combined 1,760 pages were short snippets of just twelve letters and one telegram.

Both Kelly and McFarland drew on tens of thousands of documents in the Wright Papers at the Library of Congress in Washington, D.C. When I checked there, I found well over a hundred letters by Katharine, written to her brothers and father between 1900 and 1909. After reading them, I knew that she did indeed have a story. But was there more?

and nervous and so is Orv. They will be all right when they get down in the sand. where the salt breezes blow etc. They insist that, if you aren't well enough to stay out on your trip, you must come down with them. They think that life at Kitty-Hawk cures all ills, you know.

The flying-machine is in process of making now. Will spins the sewing-machine around by the hour while Orv squats around marking the places to sew. There is no place in the house to live but I'll be lonesome enough by this time next week and wish that I could have some of their racket around.

I am enclosing the letters for you. I'd like to see Hopkins and Folk. They write such a nice letter. Will should have sent his letter to that place before you got to Obed but he didn't understand, as usual. He will write again, in a few days. Love to from you daughter

Katharine writes her father, "The flying machine is in the process of making now. . . ."
— August 20, 1902.

I found further riches at two institutions in Ohio: Wright State University in Dayton and Oberlin College in Oberlin. But the greatest resources turned up at the Western Historical Manuscript Collection in Kansas City, Missouri. In 1990 this archive microfilmed some two thousand pages written by Katharine to Henry J. (Harry) Haskell, from 1922 to 1926.

These charming, romantic, and sometimes distressing love letters illuminate every aspect of Katharine's life. Much of this book is based on insights and information gained from them. Unfortunately, very few of Harry's equally numerous letters to Katharine survive, although the Western Historical Manuscript Collection does have his unpublished autobiographical notes.

I owe a deep debt of gratitude to all of the above institutions, and especially to Dawne Dewey of Special Collections and Archives at Wright State University, Tammy L. Martin of the Oberlin College Archives, Diane Lee of the Oberlin College Library, and Jennifer S. Parker of the Western Historical Manuscript Collection.

Also helpful and a pleasure to meet via e-mail were two of Harry Haskell's grandchildren, Judith Haskell Zernich and Harry Haskell. I would also like to express my gratitude to their mother, the late Mrs. Henry C. Haskell, who loaned Katharine's letters to the Western Historical Manuscript Collection for microfilming.

Lois Walker, Wright scholar and former base historian at Wright-Patterson Air Force Base, Ohio, kindly reviewed the manuscript and made many excellent suggestions. Naturally, I am responsible for any errors that have slipped through.

Anthony Costello, M.D., of Jefferson, Massachusetts, tutored me in tuberculosis, typhoid, and other common diseases of a century ago. The staff at Gale Free Library in Holden, Massachusetts, provided crucial research materials via interlibrary loan. And my sons, Sam and Joe, rescued me from several computer emergencies.

It has been an honor to work again with agent Faith Hamlin and editor Simon Boughton. And it has been a special delight to collaborate with book designer Susan Marsh. This book is dedicated to the person who introduced Susie and me: her cousin Betty Binns Esner. Many years ago Betty gave me a job, secretly suspecting that Susie and I would hit it off — which we have, for over twenty years of happy marriage.

RICHARD MAURER
Holden, Massachusetts

Sources

THIS BOOK IS BASED on the sources listed below. For locations of specific quotes or incidents, please feel free to write me at 11 Bascom Parkway, Holden, Massachusetts 01520. I will be happy to steer you to the right spot.

LETTERS, PAPERS, DIARIES, AND RECORDS

Abbreviations:
LC: *Wright Papers, Manuscripts Division of the Library of Congress, Washington, D.C.*
OC: *Oberlin College Archives, Oberlin, Ohio*
WHMC: *Western Historical Manuscript Collection, Kansas City, Missouri*
WSU: *Wright State University Archives, Dayton, Ohio*

Arthur T. R. Cunningham: OC
Henry J. Haskell: OC, WHMC
Katharine Wright Haskell: LC, OC, WHMC, WSU
Kate B. Leonard: OC
Margaret Goodwin Meacham: OC
Harriet Silliman Myers: OC
Raymond H. Stetson: WHMC (in Katharine Wright Haskell Papers)
Lorin Wright: LC
Bishop Milton Wright: LC, WSU
Wilbur and Orville Wright: LC, WSU

WRIGHT BIOGRAPHIES, WRITINGS, ETC.

Coombs, Harry, with Martin Caidin. *Kill Devil Hill: Discovering the Secret of the Wright Brothers.* Boston: Houghton Mifflin, 1979.
Crouch, Tom. *The Bishop's Boys: A Life of the Wright Brothers.* New York: Norton, 1989.
Freudenthal, Elsbeth E. *Flight Into History: The Wright Brothers and the Air Age.* Norman: University of Oklahoma Press, 1949.

Goulder, Grace. "Katharine Wright." *Ohio Scenes and Citizens.* Cleveland: World, 1964.

Howard, Fred. *Wilbur and Orville: A Biography of the Wright Brothers.* New York: Knopf, 1987.

Jakab, Peter L. *Visions of a Flying Machine: The Wright Brothers and the Process of Invention.* Washington: Smithsonian Institution Press, 1990.

Kelly, Fred C., ed. *Miracle at Kitty Hawk: The Letters of Wilbur and Orville Wright.* New York: Farrar, Straus and Young, 1951.

———. *The Wright Brothers: A Biography Authorized by Orville Wright.* New York: Harcourt, Brace, 1943.

McFarland, Marvin W., ed., *The Papers of Wilbur and Orville Wright: Including the Chanute-Wright Letters and Other Papers of Octave Chanute,* 2 vols. New York: McGraw-Hill, 1953.

McMahon, John R. *The Wright Brothers: Fathers of Flight.* Boston: Little, Brown, 1930.

Miller, Ivonette Wright, compiler. *Wright Reminiscences.* Dayton: Air Force Museum Foundation, 1978.

Renstrom, Arthur G. *Wilbur and Orville Wright: A Chronology Commemorating the One Hundredth Anniversary of the Birth of Orville Wright.* Washington: Library of Congress, 1975.

Sullivan, Mark. "The Airplane Emerges." *Our Times: The United States, 1900–1925.* Vol. 2, Chap. 28. New York: Scribner's, 1927.

Walsh, John Evangelist. *One Day at Kitty Hawk: The Untold Story of the Wright Brothers and the Airplane.* New York: Crowell, 1975.

Wright, Bishop Milton. *Diaries, 1857–1917.* Dayton: Wright State University, 1999.

Wright, Wilbur and Orville. *The Published Writings of Wilbur and Orville Wright.* Edited by Peter L. Jakab and Rick Young. Washington: Smithsonian Institution Press, 2000.

BACKGROUND

Banner, Lois W. *Women in Modern America: A Brief History.* San Diego: Harcourt Brace Jovanovich, 1984.

Brewer, Griffith. *Fifty Years of Flying.* London: Air League of the British Empire, 1946.

Brown, Elmer E. *The Making of Our Middle Schools: An Account of the Development of Secondary Education in the United States.* New York: Longmans, Green, 1903.

Cellarius, Frederick J., compiler. *Dayton Data: Facts and Information Regarding the Gem City of Ohio.* Dayton: Cellarius, 1906.

Chanute, Octave. *Progress in Flying Machines.* New York: Forney, 1894.

Crawford, Mary Caroline. *The College Girl of America: And the Institutions Which Make Her What She Is.* Boston: Page, 1905.

Daskam, Josephine Dodge. *Middle Aged Love Stories.* New York: Scribner's, 1903.

Fergerson, Gerard. "To Live Poor But Healthy: Typhoid and the Politics of Public Health in Boston." Unpublished thesis, Harvard University, 1994.

Flexner, Eleanor. *Century of Struggle: The Women's Rights Movement in the United States.* Cambridge: Belknap Press of Harvard University Press, 1975.

Gibbs-Smith, Charles H. *The Rebirth of European Aviation, 1902–1908.* London: Her Majesty's Stationery Office, 1974.

"Had Fame But No Protection." *New York Times,* June 3, 1912.

Hi-O-Hi [Oberlin College yearbook]: *'96, '97, '97 (Vol. VIII)* [i.e., '98], *'99.* Oberlin: 1895–1898. Yearbooks from this era are generally titled with the class year of juniors who edited the volume.

Keeler, Harriet L. *The Life of Adelia A. Field Johnston Who Served Oberlin College for Thirty-Seven Years . . . .* Cleveland: Britton Printing Co., 1912.

Kinnane, Adrian J. "A House United: Morality and Invention in the Wright Brothers' Home." *The Psychohistory Review,* Vol. 16, No. 3 (Spring 1988).

Krug, Edward A. *The Shaping of the American High School.* New York: Harper & Row, 1964.

McGuffey, William H. *McGuffey's New Sixth Eclectic Reader: Exercises in Rhetorical Reading, With Introductory Rules and Examples.* Cincinnati: Wilson, Hinkle, 1867.

Memories of the World's Greatest Exposition, St. Louis, 1904. Grand Rapids: Bayne, 1904.

Millikan, Robert A. *Autobiography.* New York: Prentice-Hall, 1950.

"Miss Katherine [sic] Wright is to Wed Henry J. Haskell, *Kansas City Star* Editor." *Dayton Journal,* November 20, 1926.

Odegard, Peter H. *Pressure Politics: The Story of the Anti-Saloon League.* New York: Columbia University Press, 1928.

Orton, James. *The Liberal Education of Women.* New York: Garland, 1986.

"Orville Wright Arrives." *Kansas City Star,* March 3, 1929.

Rittenhouse, Jessie B. *The Door of Dreams.* Boston: Houghton Mifflin, 1918.

Smuts, Robert W. *Women and Work in America.* New York: Schocken, 1971.

"Speaker [Charlotte Carr] Cites Skepticism On Wrights." *Dayton Daily News,* February 1, 1948.

Timberlake, James H. *Prohibition and the Progressive Movement, 1900–1920.* Cambridge: Harvard University Press, 1963.

Woody, Thomas. *A History of Women's Education in the United States,* Vol. 2. New York: Science Press, 1929.

Index

QUOTATIONS Quotations from the Katharine Wright Haskell Papers and from the Henry C. Haskell Papers at the Western Historical Manuscript Collection, University of Missouri, Kansas City, are reprinted by permission. Quotations from *Diaries, 1857–1917* by Bishop Milton Wright and from Katharine Wright's letters to Agnes Osborn Beck are reprinted by permission of Wright State University.

PHOTOS Photo credits are listed below by page number with the following abbreviations: Images from the Prints and Photographs Division of the Library of Congress are listed by identification numbers prefaced "LC." Images from the Archives Division of the National Air and Space Museum, Smithsonian Institution, are listed by negative numbers prefaced "SI." Images from the Wright State University Archives are listed by negative numbers prefaced "WSU." **FRONT COVER:** WSU 2672; **SPINE:** WSU 829; **1:** LC-DIG-ppprs-00616; **2 (INSET):** WSU 3668; **2–3:** LC-DIG-ppprs-00666; **4–5:** WSU 2672; **6–7:** LC-DIG-ppprs-00533; **8–9:** LC-DIG-ppprs-00626; **10:** WSU 829; **13 (TOP LEFT):** LC-DIG-ppprs-00680; **13 (TOP RIGHT):** LC-DIG-ppprs-00683; **13 (BOTTOM):** WSU 2371; **15:** SI A18853; **16:** LC-DIG-ppprs-00524; **18:** LC-MSS-46706-5; **20–21:** LC-DIG-ppprs-00496; **23 (TOP):** WSU 204; **23 (BOTTOM):** WSU 2514; **24 (LEFT):** WSU 522; **24 (RIGHT):** SI A4441B; **26 (LEFT):** LC-DIG-ppprs-00540; **26 (RIGHT):** LC-DIG-ppprs-00471; **29:** LC Digital ID http://hdl.loc.gov/loc.pnp/pan.6a08541; **30:** WSU 3664; **32:** *Hi-O-Hi '97 (Vol. VIII)*, page 66; **33:** courtesy Harry Haskell; **35:** *Hi-O-Hi '96*, page 124; **36:** WSU 383; **37:** WSU 3667; **40 (TOP):** LC-DIG-ppprs-00531; **40 (BOTTOM):** LC-DIG-ppprs-00522; **41 (LEFT):** LC-DIG-ppprs-00490; **41 (TOP RIGHT):** LC-DIG-ppprs-00470; **41 (BOTTOM RIGHT):** LC-DIG-ppprs-00532; **47:** LC-DIG-ppprs-00546; **48 (LEFT):** LC-DIG-ppprs-00580; **48 (RIGHT):** LC-DIG-ppprs-00631; **49 (LEFT):** LC-DIG-ppprs-00602; **49 (RIGHT):** LC-DIG-ppprs-00614; **50–51:** WSU 3666; **53:** *Memories of the World's Greatest Exposition, St. Louis, 1904* [plate 1]; **55:** LC-DIG-ppprs-00621; **57:** LC-DIG-ppprs-00658; **66:** SI A42555C; **67:** SI NAS42667E; **71:** WSU 649; **73:** SI 85-10845; **74:** WSU 369; **75 (LEFT):** SI 93-7192; **75 (RIGHT):** WSU 482; **77:** WSU 2440; **79:** WSU 575; **80:** LC-DIG-ppprs-00715; **83:** SI A38831; **90–91:** LC-DIG-ppprs-00745; **92:** LC-DIG-ppprs-00756; **94:** WSU 2166; **95:** LC-USZ62-25103; **98:** courtesy Harry Haskell; **99 (LEFT):** courtesy Judith Haskell Zernich; **99 (RIGHT):** courtesy Harry Haskell; **101:** Oberlin College Archives, Oberlin, Ohio; **102:** Oberlin College Archives, Oberlin, Ohio; **108:** WSU 3665; **116:** LC-DIG-ppprs-00588; **119:** Oberlin College Archives, Oberlin, Ohio; **121:** Wright Papers, Manuscripts Division of the Library of Congress

SQUARE
FISH

An imprint of Macmillan Publishing Goup, LLC.
120 Broadway, New York, NY 10010
mackids.com

Our books may be purchased in bulk for promotional, educational, or business use. Please
contact your local bookseller or the Macmillan Corporate and Premium Sales Department at
(800) 221-7945 ext. 5442 or by e-mail at MacmillanSpecialMarkets@macmillan.com.
Library of Congress Cataloging-in-Publication Data
Maurer, Richard, 1950-
The Wright sister / Richard Maurer. p. cm.
Summary: Presents a brief biography of the sister of Orville and Wilbur Wright.
1. Haskell, Katharine Wright, 1874–1929—Juvenile literature. 2. Wright, Wilbur, 1867–1912—Juvenile literature. 3. Wright, Orville, 1871–1948—Juvenile literature. 4. Sisters—United States—Biography—Juvenile literature. 5. Air pilots—United States—Biography—Juvenile literature.
ISBN 978-1-250-07343-3 (paperback) [1. Haskell, Katharine Wright, 1874–1929. 2. Wright, Wilbur, 1867–1912. 3. Wright, Orville, 1871–1948. 4. Women—Biography.] I. Title.
TL540.W7 M378 2003 629.13'0092'273—dc21 2002151080

Originally published in the United States by Roaring Brook Press. First Square Fish Edition: 2016.
Book designed by Susan Marsh. Square Fish logo designed by Filomena Tuosto. AR:5.0 / LEXILE: 10l0L

9   10   8